TRUE CRIME : ILLINOIS

TRUE CRIME: ILLINOIS

The State's Most Notorious Criminal Cases

Troy Taylor

STACKPOLE
BOOKS

Published by
STACKPOLE BOOKS
5067 Ritter Road
Mechanicsburg, PA 17055
www.stackpolebooks.com

Printed in the United States of America

10 9 8 7 6 5 4 3 2 1

FIRST EDITION

Cover design by Caroline Stover

Cover photo of handgun, © Dario Sabljak/Shutterstock

Library of Congress Cataloging-in-Publication Data

Taylor, Troy.
    True crime, Illinois : the state's most notorious criminal cases /
Troy Taylor. — 1st ed.
        p.   cm.
    Includes bibliographical references.
    ISBN-13: 978-0-8117-3562-9 (pbk.)
    ISBN-10: 0-8117-3562-1 (pbk.)
    1. Crime—Illinois—Case studies. 2. Criminals—Illinois—Case studies.
I. Title.
HV6793.I3T39   2009
364.109773—dc22

2008035257

Contents

Introduction

Illinois was, in many ways, born in blood. From the Indian massacres that occurred before it was officially a state to the feuds and vendettas of the late 1800s, Illinois has a long history of violence and death. But almost every part of the country, in its early days of scant population, has been the scene of open crime. Outlaws, fleeing in desperation from the restraints of civilization, where the law was strictly enforced, found the wilderness a region where they could carry on their lawless ways. The settlements in those days were small and widely scattered, with broad spaces of unknown forest and prairie lying in between. The beleaguered upholders of the law, if they existed at all, were unable to be everywhere at once. It was easy in those days for criminals to operate in secrecy, while the very life of the frontier bred a class of rough and desperate men, capable of committing almost any crime.

There is likely no part of Illinois that does not have a local tradition of outlawry during its period of early settlement. These tales, which are often weird and gruesome, extend over many years, until the time came when popular sentiment became too strong against harboring criminals. Some locations even today are pointed out as murder sites and places where gangs of outlaws once hid. Often these tales are so filled with lore that it is hard to tell where truth ends and fiction begins. Regardless, they paint a vivid portrait of how Illinois came to be and why it gained such a reputation as a lawless place.

CHAPTER 1

A Brief History of
Crime in Illinois

Legends of death plague the rivers of Illinois—tales of bloodshed, piracy, and murder. Violence was commonplace along the rivers, where acts of piracy were frequent and often accompanied by killings. Groups of travelers were sometimes attacked in force, and the solitary man was often fortunate to escape with his life.

Many bands of pirates operated from the Wabash to the Fever River, but some of the most notorious prowled the Mississippi River from north of St. Louis to the southern tip of Illinois. During the early half of the 1800s, the confluence of the Illinois and Missouri Rivers was haunted by bands of desperadoes who found safe hiding places on the seldom-visited islands or in the well-hidden points along the shore. They often attacked travelers on both land and water and always paid special attention to the ore boats that came down-river from Galena. Their captains claimed that it was like running a gauntlet to safely make it to St. Louis. On many occasions in the early days, these pirates operated alongside the local Indians, who assisted them in their raids and gave them safe haven in their villages. Many of these outlaws also dabbled in counterfeiting, a common crime of the day, and often added murder to their lesser crimes.

Perhaps the most dangerous place along the Mississippi was the area near present-day Grand Tower, where a menacing collection of outcroppings marked a place of death for river travelers. The Native Americans were convinced that evil spirits lurked here, waiting to claim the lives of unwitting victims. The whites who settled the area later acknowledged these beliefs by giving the towering rocks a suitable name. One landmark, a rocky ridge about half a mile long, is called the Devil's Backbone. At the north edge of the Backbone is a steep gap and then the Devil's Bake Oven, a larger rock that stands on the edge of the river and rises to a height of nearly 100 feet.

The river ran red with blood there even before the river pirates began preying on passing travelers. In 1786, a band of immigrants was ascending the Mississippi River from the Ohio when they were attacked by Indians at the south edge of the Devil's Backbone. The settlers were scalped, mutilated, and killed—all except one. The only survivor was a young man named John Casper Moredock, who was able to hide in the rocks until the killers had departed. He buried his family and then made his way upstream to Kaskaskia, where he related his horrifying story and assembled a group of men who agreed to help him wreak vengeance on the Indians who took his family's life.

Moredock's party traveled south to the ambush site but was unsuccessful in finding the guilty parties. However, Moredock was unwilling to give up, and two years after the massacre, he attacked and killed a group of Indians near the massacre site. Whether these particular Indians were involved in the bloody ambush is unknown, but by this time, Moredock didn't care. As far as he was concerned, all Indians were guilty, and he began a relentless campaign to kill as many as he could. He stalked and killed dozens of Indians, many of them unarmed, and later, as the head of a volunteer militia, he reportedly shot and killed Native Americans who had surrendered to his troops. Word spread of his obsession, and he became known as the "Indian Slayer."

In the years that followed the Moredock Massacre, river navigation came to the Mississippi, and keelboats and flatboats passed the area in great numbers. According to early records, the rapids along the Backbone caused many problems for pilots when the river was in its low stages. Crews often had to disembark and walk along the shore, using ropes to pull their boats through the rapids. When going downstream, it was often necessary to reverse the process and use the long ropes to ease the boats carefully along.

During the steamboat days, the Backbone served as a landmark for river pilots, and it afforded an excellent lookout point from which boats could be seen coming for miles away. The two outcroppings of rocks also made excellent hiding places for river pirates to wait for their victims to come along. In fact, the raids by pirates became so bad that in 1803, a detachment of U.S. cavalrymen was dispatched to drive the outlaws from the area. They set up camp at the Devil's Bake Oven from May to September of that year. While the soldiers waited, the river pirates simply moved their camp to a rock overhang on the Big Muddy River; the place is still known today as Sinner's Harbor. Once the military left, the pirates returned to attacking boats on the Mississippi. Later on, as settlers and a semblance of civilization arrived, the pirates moved on, and the rapids beneath the Devil's Backbone became a much safer place.

The greatest danger to travelers and settlers during the early days of the state was the threat of robbery and murder. Bandits and highwaymen prowled the roadways, especially in the sparsely populated areas. These regions were often the scene of open crime. The persistent myth of the "good old days" in which our ancestors lived finds little support in the annals of Illinois crime during the early and middle 1800s.

No county was safe from organized outlawry in the state's early years. In 1819, a western traveler wrote: "Illinois is the hiding place for villains from every part of the United States and, indeed, from every quarter of the globe. A majority of the settlers have been discharged from penitentiaries and jails or have been the victims of misfortune or imprudence. Many of those will reform, but many, very many, are made fit for robbery and murder."

This may have been a bit of an overstatement, but it is clear that crimes of violence were alarmingly prevalent. The chief crime among them was robbery, and Illinois during the 1840s and 1850s was infested by organized bands of cutthroats who brought terror to travelers and law-abiding citizens all over the region. The two things most commonly sought were horses and money. Murder often occurred, although it was unlikely in connection to horse theft. Horses were easily passed on to confederates in some section remote from the crime for disposal to innocent buyers. The victim only knew that he had been robbed and had a slim chance of tracing his property, or of proving ownership if he did.

The stealing of money involved either robbery from individuals or theft from homes. In the latter cases, the method of operation was simple. There was a widespread mistrust of banks in those days, and people with extra funds usually hid them somewhere in their homes. This circumstance was likely to be known, or at least suspected, by neighbors, who also knew the plans of the potential victim's house and the members of the family. Any neighbor with criminal inclinations—and they were not hard to find—could pass this information on to a professional bandit, and equipped with it, the villain could commit the robbery and depart the area after paying off the neighbor for his or her part in the crime. If all went well, the crime would be one of simple burglary, but if some member of the household chanced to interrupt it, a murder was likely to follow.

Crime affected everyone in the region at that time, but strangers and travelers were especially in danger. A man might be robbed and killed in the settlement where he lived, but this could hardly be done without its becoming known to his friends and neighbors, who were likely to alert the authorities and bring about whatever justice was available at the time. A traveler from some distant place, however, was almost completely cut off from all who knew him. If his appearance or conversation were such to make people think he had a lot of money, he made a promising potential victim to the criminals who inhabited the taverns and highways. Such a person was liable to vanish without any explanation, and no one would be the wiser.

The records of the time make it painfully clear that a traveler had to be worried about his safety. One gang of outlaws whose headquarters was southwest of Chicago finally fled the country but left a number of chilling items behind. Among the effects found abandoned in the house were a suspiciously large number of trunks, cases, and empty containers that had once belonged to travelers, peddlers, and businessmen. This discovery was generally believed to account for the fate of salesmen and other travelers who, at various times, had been known to come into the community and mysteriously vanish from sight.

Samuel J. Low, who was twice elected the sheriff of Cook County in the 1840s, wrote: "Organized bands of counterfeiters, horse thieves and desperate men, versed in crime of every character abounded. For every head of the serpent crushed, another was raised. Every grove to the Wabash might have been said to contain caches of stolen goods and horses, and the cellar of many tavern the bones of murdered men."

Many outlaws, scattered about the countryside, connected themselves to the desperate gangs that operated in every corner of the state. The rough hills of southern Illinois contained many rendezvous for such robber bands, including a place called the River House in Grafton, located near the Illinois and Mississippi Rivers. It was at the River House that the killers and thieves were often harbored from the law. It was just one of twenty-six saloons that operated in Grafton in those days, and the atmosphere was so violent that it was known by the gruesome nickname of the Bloody Bucket. It was not unusual for bodies of hapless gamblers and innocent victims to be found in the woods around this bloodsoaked establishment.

The reputation for murder at the River House was widely known. One triple murder took place over the payment for stolen horses. Three men from Grafton were delivering the horses to some outlaws and decided to argue over the amount of money they were being offered for them. The outlaws made no comment. They simply shot the three men and dumped their bodies into the Illinois River.

Over the years, dozens of other such incidents occurred, including two men that were hanged from the rafters in the upstairs sleeping quarters. It was said that when the River House was torn down in 1910, bloodstains were found throughout the place, on the stairs, the walls, and splashed on the backdoor. When the wrecking crew came, they even found a noose still swinging from the rafters on the upper floor.

During the 1840s and 1850s, outlaw gangs were so rampant in Illinois that they formed regular routes of travel along the entire length of the state. For many years, the legal authorities were utterly powerless to convict them, owing to the wide influence the outlaws exercised in the towns and communities where they made their homes and freely spent their ill-gotten gains. Pitched battles between the bandits and officers of the law frequently took place. The outlaws murdered witnesses to keep them from testifying and even burned courthouses to destroy evidence. Many counties spent months in a state of terror. These events continued unchecked until honest settlers started to form bands of Regulators, vigilante societies that hanged or drove out the worst offenders.

Regulators and other vigilante groups began to appear in every corner of the state as early as 1816, for the purpose of ridding the country of undesirable characters. Though civilians taking the law into their own hands has never been endorsed, these men were largely justified by the circumstances. The entire region had been nearly overrun by counterfeiters, horse thieves, highway robbers, and killers, and no traveler was safe and no settler felt sure that his livestock would still be in their pens after a dark night. In some cases, robbers invaded small towns in search of plunder; they held up isolated merchants at gunpoint. In many counties, the outlaws were so numerous and well organized that they openly defied the law. Sheriffs, justices of the peace, judges, and constables numbered among the lawbreakers, and numerous friends in high places shielded them from punishment. When arrested, they escaped easily from poorly constructed jails, bribed the jury, or used lying witnesses to prove themselves innocent. Conviction, by any usual procedure, was practically impossible.

It was under these intolerable conditions that the people finally took the law into their own hands. The governor and most of the judges in the region, realizing the necessity of such an action, largely ignored the situation, and for a time, lynch law ruled the entire state and purged it of a great deal of the crime. These groups of Regulators, as Governor Thomas Ford described them, were in numbers about equal to companies of soldiers, and their officers were elected as in the militia. Their operations were conducted almost entirely at night, and when they assembled for duty, they marched, armed and equipped as if for war. They went to the residence or hideout of a criminal and arrested, tried, and punished him on the spot. The usual punishments were whippings and banishment from the region, although in many instances offenders were promptly hanged from the nearest tree.

In most districts, this method worked well, but for many years, a large gang of outlaws held almost absolute control over Pope, Massac, and other counties along the Ohio River and resisted every effort to dislodge them. They even built a fort of considerable strength in Pope County and openly defied the law. It was not until 1831 that measures were taken that led to their destruction. Honest settlers from all over the area banded together with weapons and attacked the outlaws' fort, even using a borrowed piece of artillery. The place was taken by sheer force, leaving three of the outlaws and one of the Regulators dead. The remaining bandits were taken prisoner and tried for their crimes.

Northern Illinois was not free from outlaw gangs and violence. Well-organized bands operated for many years north of the Illinois

River, engaging in murder, horse stealing, robbery, and counterfeiting. While few areas were completely free of criminals, the largest groups of them congregated in Ogle, Winnebago, Lee, and DeKalb Counties. In Ogle County, they became so numerous and so powerful that any conviction for crime was rendered impossible.

In the spring of 1841, seven well-known outlaws were confined in the Ogle County Jail. The judge and lawyers involved in their cases had assembled in the town of Oregon to hold proceedings in the new courthouse that had just been completed there. A gang of outlaw sympathizers set fire to the new building during the night, hoping, in all the excitement that followed, to rescue the prisoners. The jailbreak failed, but the new courthouse was completely destroyed. The public was outraged, and taking advantage of this, the court convened, and three of the prisoners were tried, convicted, and sentenced to the penitentiary. During the trial, one of the outlaws' confederates managed to get on the jury and refused to agree on a verdict until the other jury members threatened to hang him in the jury room. The four other prisoners obtained changes of venue and were never brought to trial. They managed to break out of jail and escape.

The entire affair so aroused the law-abiding citizens of the area that they resolved to take the law into their own hands. They were determined that insecure jails, changes of venue, hung juries, and perjurious evidence should no longer protect criminals from justice. All over Ogle and Winnebago Counties, vigilance committees were created, and these companies of Regulators set to work hunting down criminals, punishing them, and forcing them out of the region.

One of the worst areas in the state was Massac County, which for years was not only overrun by violent lawlessness, but actually controlled by criminals. The courts and nearly all the county and township officials were at one time actual participants in criminal behavior. In 1846, these conditions were at their height. During the summer of that year, a gang of desperadoes from Massac County went on a raid into Pope County, breaking into the home of an elderly man and robbing him of more than $2,500 worth of gold. While committing this crime, one of the bandits left behind a knife that identified him as one of the culprits. After he was arrested and tortured by angry neighbors, the bandit confessed his crime and gave them a list of his confederates. These men were also captured and tortured, and they provided other names of criminals who were scattered through various counties. A band of Regulators was organized to drive these men out, but before it could act, the election for county officers occurred in August 1846.

Every criminal influence in Massac County united for this election, and as a result, men were elected who were popularly believed to be favorable to the lawless element. Whether true or not, the two defeated candidates for sheriff and county clerk took advantage of this general feeling of mistrust to rally behind them all of the Regulator bands in Pope and Massac Counties. Assisted by numerous recruits from Kentucky, these men proceeded to punish and drive out all the suspected criminals in the area. They also tortured many of their captives to obtain the names of other possible outlaws. The usual mode of torture was to drag them down to the Ohio River and hold them underwater until they confessed. A few of these victims swore out warrants against the Regulators, but when the sheriff attempted to make arrests, he and the county clerk were both ordered to leave the area—or suffer the same fate.

By September 1846, the entire county was in the hands of the Regulators. Having been founded as a means to achieve law and order, the organization had become, under questionable leadership, a lawless terror itself, threatening everyone, whether criminal or honest man, who dared to protest against them. A reign of terror followed. In addition to the sheriff and the county clerk, several of the representatives in the legislature were driven out by force. Violence connected to the Regulators became a daily occurrence, and few dared stand against them. When the circuit court was held in Massac County, several Regulators were indicted, and some were arrested and put into jail. The Regulators, assisted by men from Kentucky, rose in open revolt against the law, and the sheriff was unable to raise enough honest men to stand against them. The Regulators took advantage of this situation and, in their full strength, marched into the county seat of Metropolis. The sheriff and his meager opposition were forced to surrender, the jail was opened, and the imprisoned Regulators were set free. Most of the sheriff's opposing force was murdered, which finally sparked a few men to organize against the Regulators. Soon the region was divided into two warring factions, known as Regulators and Flatheads. They ignored the law, and violence was commonplace. Soon no one's life or property was safe in Massac or Pope County, and the government had no way of enforcing the law.

The worst incident occurred later that year, when the Regulators attacked a man named Mathis, planning to compel him to testify against his neighbors, who were accused criminals. About twenty men came to his house one night, but Mathis and his wife resisted. Both were beaten and the wife was shot and left for dead. Mathis was carried away and probably murdered, because he was never heard from again. Warrants were sworn out against the Regulators, and ten of them were arrested. They were taken to Metropolis and placed under heavy guard by law officers and a company of Flatheads. Almost immediately, a large force of Regulators gathered and marched on Metropolis. They attacked the Metropolis House, where the prisoners were being held, and one man was fatally stabbed. The Flatheads were overpowered, and a number of them, including the sheriff, were turned over as prisoners to the Kentuckians who had assisted in the attack. The men were taken away and never heard from again.

The state of terror in this region continued undisturbed until it eventually died out naturally. The legislature made some halfhearted attempts to quell the problem, including sending in a few companies of militia, but nothing was done that accomplished any worthwhile results. No one was ever legally punished for any of the outrages committed, but the disturbances slowly died away, and law gradually returned to the area.

CHAPTER 2

The Outlaws of Cave-in-Rock

In the rough and unsettled lands of the western territories, outlaws and pirates soon emerged to prey on the travelers who journeyed down the Ohio River. Many of them established hideouts and settlements along the riverbanks. Perhaps the most famous of these locations was a place called Cave-in-Rock, in the southeastern corner of Illinois. The cave became a stronghold for pirates who plundered flatboats on the river and murdered and robbed travelers. It was also here, around 1800, that thieves began operating a tavern and gambling parlor in the cave, using whiskey, cards, and prostitutes to lure travelers in off the river. Many of these customers wound up beaten and robbed, and sometimes murdered, after tying up at the crude wharf. Dozens, perhaps hundreds, of westward travelers vanished without a trace from the river near this cave—and were never heard from again.

During the early 1800s, many pioneers used the Ohio River to begin their travels to the West. It was a simple way to move wagons, people, and goods and eat up huge chunks of the westward trail. Travel by river was anything but serene, however. Besides the danger of the pirates, thieves, and Indians, the river was filled with hazards like floating logs and "sweepers," fallen trees with branches that extended out into the water. These often were embedded in the mud and lay just below the surface of the water, making them invisible to the boat pilots. If the flatboats hit these obstacles, it could take hours to repair the damage. Other dangers included floods, unexpected currents, eddies in the river, and even storms that could easily sink a boat.

But these natural hazards were nothing compared with what lurked in the dark corners of Cave-in-Rock. From this vantage point, the pirates could see for many miles up the Ohio River. The unusual cave in the massive rock bluff often called to weary travelers like a beacon, but when a flatboat got near the shore, pirates were liable to board the vessel, kill everyone on board, and then scuttle the craft after stealing all of the cargo. In those days, the cave boasted a partially concealed entrance and a wide view up and down the river. It was about 200 feet long and 80 feet wide, with a level floor and a vertical chimney that ascended to the bluff above.

The cave was originally used by Native Americans, but the whites soon claimed it for more nefarious uses. Around 1800, a man named Wilson brought his family to live in the cave, and he turned it into a dwelling and a tavern. He erected a sign along the water's edge that read, "Wilson's Liquor Vault & House of Entertainment." The novelty of the place attracted river travelers, and it soon became a rough spot, famed for its hard cider, whiskey, and women of ill repute.

A band of robbers formed by Wilson became the first pirates to operate on this stretch of the river. These pirates killed whole crews of boats on their way to New Orleans when they docked at the cave, and then stole and sold their cargo. After many months of robberies, the tavern became known from Pittsburgh to New Orleans as a place to avoid, and public indignation forced the authorities to finally act. Many of the pirates were arrested, but others were killed or fled the region. Wilson was murdered at the hands of his own men when they learned of the huge reward that had been placed on his head. There is, as they say, no honor among thieves. After Wilson's death, more than sixty bodies of luckless travelers were discovered hidden away in an upper room of the cave.

Samuel Mason was the next outlaw connected with Cave-in-Rock. Mason was a man who killed for both pleasure and profit. He operated along the Mississippi River and on the fabled Natchez Trace, a series of trails in the south that became known as a haven for thieves and pirates. But he was not always a lawless man. Mason had been an officer in Washington's army during the Revolutionary War. He had served with distinction, was promoted to captain, and was cited twice for bravery.

During the war, he came west to Kentucky and joined George Rogers Clark in the raid on Vincennes. While in the Illinois region, he became acquainted with John Duff at Fort Massac. Duff was a scout for Clark, but he was believed to be a double agent, also acting as a spy for the British. He later became a skilled counterfeiter and a brother-in-law to Samuel Mason. After the capture of Vincennes in February 1779, Mason returned to Fort Henry in Virginia and served with Colonel Daniel Brodhead against the Seneca Indians in August of that same year. He operated a tavern in Wheeling for a time, but after running afoul of the law, he came west to Kentucky. He lived there for a year or so but had to leave after falling under suspicion for three murders. His next stop was Cave-in-Rock.

Mason took over Wilson's tavern and renamed it the Rock Cave Inn. Women and whiskey became the drawing cards to lure travelers to the inn. He adopted Wilson's methods of piracy as well. He often had a prostitute who worked for him stand on the shore and pretend to be stranded. When a boat came to pick her up, the pirates would swarm over the craft, seizing the cargo and murdering the crew. Mason's pirates also posed as legitimate river pilots who could be hired to steer vessels along a dangerous channel that ran nearby. On rainy nights, welcoming lanterns were placed along the riverbanks in order to lure boats that were being tossed about in the storm to put ashore. Just before the boat reached the bank, it would plow into a sandbar or a line of rocks. The stranded vessel would then be overrun by Mason's cutthroats.

Still another approach was one that was most frequently used by Mason's most fearsome confederates, Micajar and Wiley Harpe. The Harpe brothers, known as "Big Harpe" and "Little Harpe," were remorseless butchers whose victims included innocent women and children. Big Harpe once admitted to smashing a newborn baby against a tree because her crying annoyed him. The Harpes operated boldly in broad daylight. Their most effective method was to appear on the riverbank and flag down passing boats, usually saying that they had been attacked by Indians or robbed, and needed help. When the sympathetic travelers came ashore, the Harpes slaughtered them on the spot and raided the boat. The Harpes disemboweled their victims, loaded their stomachs with stones, and then sank them in the river.

As it later turned out, the Harpes were too vile for even the rough outlaws at Cave-in-Rock. After a raid on a flatboat, the sole survivor of the craft was stripped of his clothes, tied onto a blindfolded horse, and run off a cliff while the Harpes watched and laughed with delight. The other outlaws who witnessed this were sickened by the brothers' bloodthirsty entertainment and made the Harpes and their women leave. Not long after, Big Harpe met his end. He and his brother murdered the wife of Moses Stegall, cut her baby's throat, and then set the house on fire to conceal the crime. Stegall quickly formed a posse. Little Harpe managed to escape, but John Leiper shot Big Harpe in the spine, leaving him paralyzed. John Stegall beheaded him as he lay on his deathbed, but Big Harpe never begged for his life. He simply growled, "Cut away and be damned." Big Harpe's head was placed on a stake and left outside the ruins of the Stegall house as a warning to other outlaws.

THE OUTLAWS OF CAVE-IN-ROCK

Samuel Mason was eventually driven out of the Cave-in-Rock area, and he took up operations on the Mississippi and along the Natchez Trace. He amassed a fortune during the five years or so that his criminal enterprise flourished in the region, but he did not survive to spend it. After the United States purchased the Louisiana Territory from France, a concerted effort was made to drive out the outlaw element that had existed along the river for years. The authorities placed a reward on Mason's head, offering $10,000 for his capture, dead or alive.

Wiley Harpe was the man who finally killed Samuel Mason. He contrived to get Mason alone, and then Little Harpe buried his tomahawk into his friend's back. He finished him off and hacked off Mason's head. He carried the grisly object off and placed it on the desk of the judge who had been charged with dispensing the reward. The men who were present that day all confirmed that it was the head of Samuel Mason, but just as the judge was counting out the gold coins in payment, one of the bystanders recognized Little Harpe as an outlaw himself. Harpe made an effort to escape, but he was quickly captured and hanged soon after. The deaths of Mason and Harpe brought about the end of the gang, and Mason's men scattered to the winds.

Around 1830, Billy Potts and his wife began operating a tavern near Cave-in-Rock, which was known as the Potts' Inn. Their only son, also named Billy, threw in with the outlaws who were operating along the river and as a young man was already an accomplished thief. He was so merciless that he even preyed on the travelers who came to his parents' tavern. He lured unsuspecting customers out to a spring near the building and robbed them after slicing them open with his knife. The easy money soon became too great of a temptation to his parents, and they began assisting in his crimes. His mother often helped dismember the murder victims, and his father buried the pieces in an abandoned well and in shallow graves on their property.

Young Billy later ran afoul of the law and decided to leave the area. He was gone for several years, and while away, he gained weight and grew a beard. When he felt that it was safe to come home and visit his parents, he traveled back and showed up at his family's tavern. He had changed so much that his mother did not recognize him, but she did see the heavy bag of loot he had with him. After eating, Billy went outside to drink from the spring, and his father sprang out of the shadows and stabbed him, thinking he was just another traveler. The body was hastily buried in a shallow grave in the woods.

The next day, several members of Billy's old gang showed up looking for their friend. One of them asked Mrs. Potts how she liked having her son home again, and she nearly collapsed in shock. She and her husband quickly exhumed the body they had buried the night before, unable to believe they had robbed and murdered their own son. It is said that Mrs. Potts collapsed when she recognized his body from a birthmark.

They abandoned their life of crime but never really recovered from what had happened. Mrs. Potts painted an image of her son's face on the rock that overlooked the spring on their property, and it remains there to this day, although it has faded over the years. It lingers as a tragic reminder of a woman's grief and a wasted life that ended in murder.

Counterfeiters, or "coiners," as they were called in those days, also operated at Cave-in-Rock for many years. During the American Revolution, the British flooded the new country with counterfeit Continental currency. This weakened the government, and it also gave outlaws a new method of getting rich. The Spanish-milled dollar backed up the young nation's currency before mints were opened in 1793, so foreign currency was in use for many years in America. Andrew Jackson paid off his men with the Spanish dollar during the War of 1812, and the term "bit" was commonly used in the Illinois Territory. The Spanish dollar was also known as a "piece of eight," because it was valued in eight bits. It was common to take a chisel to this coin to make smaller change, which is how terms like "two bits," for 25 cents, came into use.

Phillip Alston, a criminal from South Carolina, is believed to have brought the first coining dies to Cave-in-Rock, and there he taught John Duff, Samuel Mason's friend and brother-in-law, how to make coins. Alston had stolen a gold statue from a Catholic church in Natchez, Mississippi, and melted it with other metals to make coins. He was suspected in the theft, so he moved to Kentucky, where he ran a saltworks, store, and tavern; preached; and taught school. He also operated the first mint in Kentucky, albeit an unofficial one. When his neighbors took a dislike to his coins, he fled the area and joined Duff at Cave-in-Rock. Alston later left the region for reasons unknown and was never heard of again.

After Mason and Alston left Cave-in-Rock, Duff continued to counterfeit coins there until he was killed by Shawnee Indians in 1804. His operation was taken over by "Bloody" Jack Sturdevant, a gambler and outlaw, whose confederates scattered bogus bills and home-coined currency all over the region and beyond. Many of the fake coins were passed to travelers and those who crossed a nearby river ferry, spreading the counterfeit currency all over the country.

Sturdevant used Cave-in-Rock as his banking and distribution point. He remained in the area until 1831, when a band of Regulators became determined to drive him out of business. They attacked his headquarters, but Sturdevant managed to drive them off with a small cannon that he had procured from some river pirates. Though this stopped the attack, Sturdevant decided to leave the area anyway. Abandoning his operations, he and his men vanished under cover of darkness. He was never heard from again.

Although Samuel Mason had departed Cave-in-Rock and took up thieving and killing on the Natchez Trace, river pirates continued to operate out of the cave for years. Their operations continued under a new leader, an outwardly respectable businessman who operated a ferryboat a few miles upriver. The owner of Ford's Ferry, James Ford, was a wealthy man with extensive landholdings in both Kentucky and Illinois. He was appointed as a justice of the peace by Kentucky's governor, James Girard, and was generous to his neighbors in Illinois. He believed in education and saw to it that his daughter, Cassandra, was well schooled, something unusual for young women of the time. He cared for his family and had a genuine love for his children. He provided well for them, but his generosity did not apply to his second wife, a woman he abused and for whom he left nothing in his will.

Ford's first wife was Susan Miles, the daughter of a prosperous early settler, and together they had three children, Phillip, William, and Cassandra. His daughter was later married to Dr. Charles Webb of Princeton and was respected and admired by all who knew her. Dr. Webb repeatedly said in later years that his wife never knew Ford as anything other than a kind and loving father.

In a short period of time, from 1797 to 1818, James Ford went from poverty as a land surveyor to great wealth as a ferry operator and property owner. He maintained vast tracts of property in his own name and the names of his children. By 1818, he had acquired more than 850 acres of land in Kentucky and Illinois, as well as slaves, horses, timberland, and saltworks. Some wondered about his source of wealth, but few dared to do so aloud, fearing Ford's temper and political clout too much to make accusations of any kind.

The years following the War of 1812 were a boom time for the pirates who attacked and robbed travelers on the Ohio River. Warnings began to be issued about the riverbanks of southern Illinois, and armed guards started accompanying the boats, making piracy hazardous. But James Ford was smart enough to realize that he had to change his methods of operation to keep up with the times. This led him to start a river ferry in 1823, a whole new arm of operation for his criminal enterprise.

Now the river pirates became land robbers and murderers, seizing wagons and raiding settlers who crossed over on Ford's Ferry from Kentucky. In time, Ford owned and operated a number of ferries, but the only one connected to his illegal operations was near Cave-in-Rock. Pirates stripped and burned prosperous wagons, killing the travelers and burying them in the woods. No one was ever left alive to identify the outlaws later. Ford ran the entire operation from the background, and if any of his men were caught or suspected, he used his legal connections to get him out of the territory before they could come to trial.

After Ford's first wife died in the early 1820s, he married a widow, Elizabeth Armstead Frazer. She had come down the river with her husband and three daughters, and having known Ford in the past, they visited with him. Ford was the justice of the peace who had married her to James Frazer in 1817. While he was a houseguest of Ford's, James Frazer became stricken with a mysterious illness and died. Alone and destitute, Elizabeth reluctantly married Ford. Frequent disagreements arose, because she was not the quiet and mild woman his first wife had been. She probably suspected that Ford had something to do with her husband's death. Ford often abused Elizabeth and treated her horribly, but given the man her husband was, she was lucky her fate was not a more heinous one.

As Ford's wealth grew, more people began to wonder about the source of his money. During this time period, a number of groups of Regulators were formed in southern Illinois when local residents began to feel that organized law had failed them. It was a group of Regulators that would bring an end to James Ford's operations.

An argument between two of Ford's men set things into motion. Henry Shouse quarreled bitterly with Vincent Simpson, a former henchman of Ford's. Ford had previously sued Simpson over a slave named Hiram, whom Ford maintained had been misrepresented to him at the time of purchase. The trial was a ruse to discredit Simpson, as it was thought he was planning trouble for the outlaws. They believed that if his reputation could be besmirched, no one would take seriously any accusations that he might make against Ford. One day after a court hearing, Shouse and Simpson began fighting. Later that day, Simpson was on his way to Shouse's home with a loaded gun, but Shouse shot him first without warning. Simpson lingered for several days after the shooting and then died.

Shouse and two of his cronies, James Mulligan and William H. J. Stevenson, rode out for Arkansas but soon were captured and returned to Illinois. Shouse was indicted for murder, and his friends were named as accomplices. Mulligan later died while in jail, and Stevenson escaped. Shouse was hanged in Golconda in 1834.

Meanwhile, the Regulators decided that although Ford had managed to stay ahead of the law with his money and power, he was as guilty as his men were of the murder. One evening, a group of Regulators followed him to the home of Vincent Simpson's widow. He had gone there for dinner and allegedly to provide comfort for the woman after the recent loss of her husband. Unknown to Ford, the widow Simpson would have a hand in his murder. He was eating his food at the table when the woman brought him a candle and asked that he read a letter aloud for her. The candle had been a prearranged signal for the Regulators outside, and when they saw it, they opened fire on the house. Ford died with seventeen bullets in his body.

For years after his death, slaves told stories about how Jim Ford had died and "landed in hell headfirst." At his funeral, attended only by his widow, a few family members, and some slaves, a terrible thunderstorm came up. Just as Ford's coffin was being lowered into the ground, lightning flashed and a deafening clap of thunder filled the air, causing one of the slaves to lose his grip on the rope holding the coffin. The box dropped into the grave headfirst and wedged there at a strange angle. The heavy rain made it impossible to move the casket, so it was covered over the way it had fallen. This left Ford to spend eternity standing on his head.

Ford's death did not bring an end to the activities of the outlaws at Cave-in-Rock. Many of them moved on to other areas or stayed in the region, joining up with other operations. A number of them joined James A. Murrell in his Mystic Clan, which continued to terrorize the area.

Born between 1800 and 1804 in Tennessee, where his mother ran a tavern and his father was an itinerant preacher, Murrell embraced a life of crime during his early years. With his father gone most of the time, Murrell's mother took in criminals as boarders and turned the tavern into a combination hotel and brothel. When Murrell was sixteen, his mother took up with Daniel Crenshaw, a criminal from the Cave-in-Rock area. Crenshaw had a varied career of pushing counterfeit money for Bloody Jack Sturdevant, working as a river pirate, and selling stolen slaves. One night, while Crenshaw and his mother were in bed, Murrell used a skeleton key to steal a pistol and several other items from a locked trunk that belonged to Crenshaw. He also robbed the tavern's money box of $50 and fled.

A short time later, Murrell ran into Crenshaw in Nashville, but Crenshaw was not angry with the young man. In fact, he was delighted to see him and decided to take him under his wing and teach him the fine arts of robbery and murder. Within a week, they had killed and robbed their first man, a South Carolinian who was carrying $1,262. Murrell developed a taste for blood and became a brilliant and capable outlaw.

Caught stealing horses, Crenshaw and Murrell were arrested, convicted, and branded on their thumbs, which was the standard punishment of the day. They were also whipped before being sent to prison for a year. While incarcerated, Murrell studied the Bible and began developing a new scheme for when he was released. After he was discharged from prison, he would conduct revival meetings, and while he preached, his confederates would work their way through the crowd, stealing and picking pockets. Murrell often boasted, "I preach a damn fine sermon!"

He worked this operation for a while before coming up with a new scheme. Thanks to Crenshaw, Murrell was familiar with the Underground Railroad, a secret network that helped slaves escape from the South and journey to freedom in the North. There were a number of Underground Railroad stations near Cave-in-Rock and scattered throughout southern Illinois. Murrell was not interested in helping escaped slaves, though; he was interested only in the money he could make from the Underground Railroad. He spread the word that he was able to help slaves escape but could do so only for a high price—a price that the slaves themselves would be able to provide. He helped slaves run away and then resold them into slavery, explaining that he would use the money to help them escape again and it would pay their way to freedom. Needless to say, they never saw Murrell again. If a slave questioned this arrangement or acted suspicious, Murrell would simply kill them. Some believe that he may have killed 100 or more slaves during the time that he was running this operation.

Not long after this, Murrell started the first organized crime syndicate in the West, his Mystic Clan. When admitted to the gang, each member had to take an oath, which was signed in blood. Members also had a signal so that they could recognize each other. Twelve of Murrell's most trusted men formed the Grand Council, and the rest of the members were soldiers known as "strikers," who did most of the dirty work. Murrell listed 452 names in the Mystic Clan, a number of whom were former associates of James Ford.

Within two years of Murrell's release from prison, he had a smooth-running operation, thieving horses, robbing travelers, stealing slaves, and passing counterfeit money. But it was not to last. Murrell was arrested again around 1834 and sentenced to serve ten years in the penitentiary. He practiced blacksmithing for a time after he was released in 1845, but prisons were horrible places in those days, and Murrell's health was broken. He died within a few months of his release.

By the mid-1830s, most of the outlaws, pirates, and counterfeiters had been driven away from Cave-in-Rock, and the bloody past of the place began to fade with time. As years passed, the cave became more of a recreation area than a den of thieves, and it remains a natural attraction in southern Illinois today.

The legends have never died completely, though, and many still remember the area's bloodsoaked past. This is a place where history has certainly left its mark, and the legends of Cave-in-Rock prove that in some cases, truth really is stranger than fiction.

CHAPTER 3

Bloody Williamson County

After the War of 1812, southern Illinois began to see large numbers of American settlers, many of them coming from the southern states of North Carolina, Kentucky, Tennessee, and Virginia. They brought with them their southern ideas and traditions, which would long hold reign over the thoughts and politics of the region. For a number of years, slavery was even allowed here, as the owners of the salt mines in the southeastern corner of the state were allowed to lease slaves from Kentucky to work their holdings. The southern influence was so strong in some areas that shortly after the outbreak of the Civil War, Williamson County attempted to secede from the Union, and many of the settlers even went south to fight for the Confederacy.

The early southern settlers also brought with them the feuds and violence of the Appalachians. One feud in Johnson County, at a place called Hell's Neck, flared into a bitter conflict that cost several lives. But none could compare to Williamson County's "Bloody Vendetta." Williamson County has become well known to historians and crime enthusiasts as "Bloody Williamson"—a dark, and most likely not appreciated, nickname it earned in the 1920s after being the scene of a bloody massacre, brutal battles with the Ku Klux Klan, and a fierce Prohibition war between battling bootleggers.

Long before Prohibition, though, death came to Williamson County in the form of a bitter vendetta between two families and their supporters.

The "Bloody Vendetta" began as a tavern brawl on July 4, 1868. Several members of the Bulliner family were playing cards in a saloon with a man named Henderson. He made the mistake of calling one of the Bulliners a "damn lying son of a bitch," and in the fight that followed, Henderson was badly beaten. After that, the two families became bitter enemies and soon involved other families in the feud, including the Sisneys, Russells, and Crains. Between 1868 and 1876, the families fought out the vendetta in the barnyards, bars, and streets of Williamson County.

The Sisneys entered the vendetta a year after the first troubles began between the Bulliners and the Hendersons. George Sisney won a lawsuit against a Bulliner man over a crop of oats. Later, during a meeting to settle the affair, Bulliner accused Sisney of lying. A fight started, and soon other Bulliners were attacking the Sisney house with weapons. Sisney ran into a nearby field, and although he was hit four times by bullets, he managed to hold off the Bulliners from the cover of a large tree. The Sisneys were now involved in the feud on the side of the Hendersons, for they believed there was no way to stay out of it.

Two years later, the Crains joined the vendetta after a fight with several of the Sisneys at the general store in Carterville, and Tom

Russell also got involved. The battles continued for years, and a dozen men were either killed or wounded in the fighting.

The unluckiest of the fighters was George Sisney. After the unsuccessful attack on his home, he moved to Carbondale to get clear of the battle. A short time later, however, he was badly hurt by a shotgun blast through his living-room window. He managed to recover, but then less than a year later, he was killed by another shotgun blast.

Finally, in 1876, Marshall Crain was arrested and tried for murder, and the feud died out. After seven years of reluctance on the part of the authorities to do anything about the violence, Crain was hanged, and three others—John Bulliner, Allen Baker, and Samuel Music—were imprisoned.

Violence had become commonplace in Williamson County, but one event that occurred in June 1922 gave the county its permanent nickname. This incident, known as the "Herrin Massacre," gained national attention and left a permanent scar on the region.

The small town of Herrin is located in the heart of coal country. Rich veins of coal were discovered nearby in the late 1800s, and for a time, it became the chief source of wealth and industry in southern Illinois. Conditions for the workers were less than adequate, however, and the lives and health of the employees were of little concern to the mine owners. Men worked in water up to their knees, and in gas-filled rooms and unventilated mines where the air was filthy and filled with toxins. There was no compensation for accidents, which occurred frequently, and the average daily wage was often less than $2. Then, around 1900, the mine workers began to organize, forming unions to combat the low pay and horrible conditions. New laws were implemented, and wages grew rapidly. Standards of living finally began to rise, and small towns like Herrin began to prosper.

None of this came easily, however, and there were many struggles between the miners' unions and the mine companies, which were interested only in profits. Many of the struggles resulted in strikes and violence before the mine unions were recognized.

By the 1920s, the miners' unions were secure in southern Illinois, and at this same time, the method known as strip mining also came into practice. Here, large shovels and drag lines were used to strip the earth above coal beds that were close to the surface. In September 1921, William Lester of the Southern Illinois Coal Company opened a new strip mine about halfway between Herrin and Marion. The mine employed fifty workers, all members of the United Mine Workers of America.

On April 1, 1922, the United Mine Workers went on strike across the country, ceasing all coal-mining operations. Lester, who was deeply in debt with his new operation, was in fear of losing his company. He negotiated with the local union, which agreed to let him continue taking coal from the ground, as long as he did not try to ship it out. With this stockpile in place, Lester could ship the coal as soon as the strike ended.

By June, the union workers had dredged almost 60,000 tons of coal. The price for the product had risen considerably, thanks to the strike, and the chance for high profit was a temptation too great for Lester to withstand. He fired all of his union miners and hired fifty strikebreakers and mine guards from Chicago. On June 16, he shipped out sixteen railroad cars of coal, effectively breaking the agreement he had made at the start of the strike.

Word soon got out about what Lester was doing, and leaders of the United Mine Workers union and officials from the Illinois government tried to persuade him to stop. Miners were outraged and began to rally. In the days that followed, many tried to reason with Lester, but he refused to listen. He was contacted repeatedly by Colonel Samuel Hunter of the Illinois National Guard, who warned him that the situation he was causing could be very dangerous. Lester ignored him, as did the local sheriff, who disregarded Hunter's advice to deputize additional men in case of problems.

Rumbling continued among the local miners. On June 21, a truck carrying eleven armed guards and strikebreakers was ambushed east of Carbondale, at a bridge over the Big Muddy River. A contingent of union workers sprayed the truck with gunfire. Three men were wounded, and six others escaped by jumping into the water below the bridge.

Later that same day, several hundred miners gathered at the Herrin Cemetery and then looted several local hardware stores. The mob took all of the firearms and ammunition they could find, and then moved out to the mine site. A constant exchange of gunfire developed between the frightened strikebreakers and the angry union men. Three of the union miners were fatally shot.

Throughout the morning and early afternoon, various attempts were made to try to defuse the situation. The union men were noncommittal about working out a solution. Late in the afternoon, Colonel Hunter received a call from the mine superintendent, who explained that the mine had been surrounded and shots were being fired. The sheriff could not be located, and the superintendent begged Hunter to send troops. Soon National Guardsmen were dispatched with orders to stop the attack and disperse the miners. For some reason, the troops never arrived. Colonel Hunter stated later that he believed the strikers and the men inside the mine had made a truce. The sheriff could not be reached, and the telephone lines to the mine were cut. Regardless, Hunter still did not send out the troops.

Meanwhile, Hugh Willis, the spokesman for the United Mine Workers union in the area, arrived in Herrin and addressed the local supporters. His take on the situation was that the strikebreakers never should have come to Herrin, and whatever happened to them, they deserved. His comments further inflamed the volatile situation.

Throughout the night, strikers destroyed equipment and machinery around the mine, using dynamite, shovels, and hammers. Finally, after being begged by the strikebreakers inside, the superintendent agreed to surrender. He told the assembled strikers that they would all come out, as long as they could leave the county unharmed. The strikers agreed, and the men inside cautiously emerged from the mine.

They lined up, and the union miners began marching them toward Herrin. They began walking, stopping once when they were approached by an armed procession that threatened to kill the strikebreakers. Cooler heads apparently prevailed, and the procession continued on. The union men were angry and determined not to let the strikebreakers and guards get off without some sort of punishment. The workers particularly despised the mine superintendent, C. K. McDowell, who had previously treated the union men with arrogance and bragged that the mine would stay open whether there was a strike or not. On his forced march, McDowell was repeatedly struck and badly bloodied. His wooden leg made it difficult for him to keep pace, further infuriating his captors. After a short distance, several of the men carried McDowell off to the side and shot him twice in the chest.

The mob then marched the men a little farther, to a powerhouse for the local railroad. To the north was a section of woods. The procession stopped as an automobile drove up. According to accounts of the survivors, Hugh Willis got out and told the miners not to kill the captives on the public road; instead, he said, "Take them over to the woods and give it to them. Kill all you can."

The prisoners were then marched to the woods, near a barbed-wire fence. Shots began to ring out, and the strikebreakers ran. Some of them never made it to the fence. Others scrambled up and over it, or became terrifyingly trapped in the wire, then blasted apart by bullets. The strikebreakers, unfamiliar with the area, plunged into the woods or ran toward Herrin. The miners tracked them through the trees and continued to slay them, one by one.

One group of six men was captured and taken to the Herrin Cemetery. Here they were slaughtered in front of a crowd that contained both women and children. One miner ended the massacre by going from one wounded man to another and cutting the throats of those who remained alive. It was a scene of unbelievable horror.

During all of it, the sheriff was noticeably absent. He was eventually tracked down by National Guard officers and went to the mine site. The operation was in flames, and a trail of violence was traced by the bodies that had been left behind. Those who had not died were taken to Herrin Hospital, but at least twenty of the strike-breakers had been killed in the slaughter. The strikebreakers who died were buried in a common grave in Herrin Cemetery. Their identities remain unknown to this day.

Word quickly spread across the country about the terrible events. Newspapers and officials cried for justice to be done in the case. Editorials railed against the viciousness of the attack, congressmen took the opportunity to attack the unions, and President Warren G. Harding denounced it as "butchery . . . wrought in madness."

Area miners remained stoic and remorseless. The coroner's reports on the massacre ruled that the strikebreakers were killed by "unknown individuals" and declared that the deaths had been caused by the actions of the Southern Illinois Coal Company and not the striking miners. These findings further outraged some factions of the public, and several months later, pressure forced a grand jury to hand down indictments against six men for the murder of one of the strikebreakers. The prosecutor used eyewitness testimony from surviving workers to present his case, but the defense managed to try to justify the mob's actions. The jury acquitted all six of the defendants.

The press and public officials outside of the area were again infuriated and called for a new trial, which took place in 1923. By now public interest in the case had waned, but the prosecutor again tried the same six defendants, although this time for the murder of another strikebreaker. Reliable testimony was once again presented, but once more, the defense attorney justified the mob's actions. The jury was convinced and the defendants were again set free.

This was the last trial held, and none of the killers were ever punished for their part in the massacre. "Bloody Williamson" gained a notoriety that lingers to this day.

Prohibition turned many southern Illinoisans into bootleggers during the 1920s. With the liquor stills and illegal booze shipments came lawlessness, violence, and bloodshed. Many in the region believed that they needed more help than local law enforcement could provide and welcomed the arrival of the Ku Klux Klan in 1923. The Klan saw the discontent of the people as an opportunity to step in and provide relief, as well as their version of law and order. As most of the bootleggers were "Catholics and foreigners" anyway, this provided the Klan with the perfect opportunity.

The Klan began its movement into the county by appearing at local churches with gifts of money and speeches on law and order and "walking the line of Americanism." Such sentiment was greeted warmly by the mostly Protestant and largely uneducated residents of the county. The local officials did little to curb the lawless elements in the region, and Williamson County was ready for a "cleaning up." The Klan was now offering them a chance to put the bootleggers and the gamblers out of business and make Williamson County "more like home and less like hell."

Concerned by the growing number of Klansmen in the county, the local sheriff also made an effort to curb the violence and the liquor, going out on ineffectual raids and making token arrests. The Klan was not happy and was impatient to see something done. The county would be cleaned up, the Klansmen said, "if we have to do it ourselves."

The first move was to appeal to the Illinois governor for control. They were rebuffed but didn't stop there. A committee then went to Washington, where they met with Roy Haynes, the commissioner of Prohibition. He sympathized but could do little to help, so someone put the committee in touch with a former Prohibition agent named S. Glenn Young. The committee retained him to conduct the cleanup in Williamson County.

Young arrived in Williamson County in November 1923 and began visiting speakeasies in the county and compiling evidence against the owners. By the end of the month, Young and his men had bought illegal liquor in 100 different establishments. With such evidence in hand, Young managed to become deputized as a Prohibition agent, although later, officials in the government would deny any connection with him. Shortly after, Young began recruiting men from the Klan into his private army. He would go on to essentially become an "enforcer," making his own rules and laws for the county.

Young and his 500 recruits began a series of raids that would fill the jails in Herrin and Benton. Young decked himself out in a military uniform, with two .45s strapped to his legs, and began carrying a submachine gun. He was at once both a comical figure on a reckless quest for power—and a terrifying one. After three raids, which resulted in 256 arrests, Williamson County was in an uproar.

The raiders did not limit themselves to speakeasies either. Many of the attacks fell on private homes, and it was probably not a coincidence that most of these homes belonged to Italians and Catholics. There were stories of brutality, robbery, and even planted evidence. The Klansmen scoffed at the charges leveled against them by the "foreigners," but many concerned citizens found them convincing.

Chaos reigned in Williamson County. Most of the charges of brutality had been directed toward Young. After a fight, Young was arraigned on assault charges. During the hearing, several Klansmen stalked into the courtroom. They were heavily armed, carrying the machine guns used in their raids. The jury retired and immediately returned with a verdict of not guilty. And this was only the beginning. Shortly after the "trial," Young was also able to get the local sheriff to dismiss his deputies and hire all Klan supporters. He was essentially continuing the organization of his own personal army.

But all was not well for Young in the county. One night in Herrin, a meeting of an anti-Klan group erupted into violence when it was breached by two Klan officers, John Ford and Harold Crain. A scuffle followed, and a Klan opponent named John Layman was shot. In the confusion that followed, other Klansmen were disarmed and taken away as prisoners.

Shortly after, word of the fighting reached Caesar Cagle, a former bootlegger turned Klan supporter, who rounded up a group of men and went after the anti-Klan group. Cagle was killed shortly after, and when word spread, the Klan converged on Herrin. Hundreds of Klansmen began patrolling the city streets and stopping cars, looking for Cagle's killers. Warrants were sworn out against several of the suspects and even C. E. Anderson, the mayor of Herrin. The Klansmen headed for the hospital and demanded entrance from Dr. J. T. Black, the administrator. When he refused, the Klan opened fire on the hospital, endangering the lives of the doctors, nurses, and innocent patients.

Within hours, the National Guard had arrived and quickly dispersed the mob. The hospital was terribly damaged, with broken glass covering the floors and bullet marks pitting the walls facing every outside window. Amazingly, not a single person in the building was injured.

Young ignored the presence of the National Guard troops, and his men continued to patrol the streets wearing crude tin stars. He arrested the mayor and pretty much anyone who opposed him. He even arrested the sheriff, whom he blamed for Cagle's murder. Young then appointed himself the sheriff, and no one dared oppose him.

Thus in a little more than three months, S. Glenn Young had made himself the dictator of an American county, but it would not last. Soon officials were starting to complain about the Klan's "reign of terror."

A short time later, Young was charged with trying to overthrow the civil authorities of Williamson County, and he later moved to East St. Louis. The charges against Young were overshadowed by a number of liquor-related trials and the fact that the Klan managed to sweep the November elections, remaining in control of Williamson County.

On May 23, 1924, Young and his wife were driving to East St. Louis when a Dodge pulled up alongside them and fired a volley of bullets into the Youngs' car. Young was wounded, and his wife was blinded by the fire. Word of the attack quickly reached Klan supporters, who swore revenge. A large number of them organized and began searching for the car. Later that morning, the Dodge was spotted in Carterville, and Klansmen opened fire. The automobile ran off the road, and two men emerged from the wreckage and tried to flee. One was wounded and the other killed. The dead man was Jack Skelcher, a bootlegger. His companion, Charles Briggs, had earlier been indicted for robbery. A coroner's jury ruled that Skelcher's death had been at the hands of "unknown persons."

Young was back in the spotlight again, and he pushed for indictments in his attack. In June, he swore out warrants for attempted murder against Briggs and also against Carl and Earl Shelton, local bootleggers, who he claimed were in the Dodge with the other two men. The case never went to trial, in spite of a preliminary hearing where Young showed up with thirty carloads of armed Klansmen to identify the assailants. After that, Young continued to be involved in several altercations and in political and legal blunders that would get him indicted and forced out of the Klan.

A short time later, the court case against Caesar Cagle's killers was dismissed, leading to more violence. Half an hour after court adjourned, a number of anti-Klansmen went to Smith's garage in Herrin to demand the return of the Dodge driven by Jack Skelcher in the attack on S. Glenn Young. The incident resulted in a shootout, leaving six men dead. Three of them were Klansmen. Fearing more trouble, the National Guard was again dispatched.

In the meantime, Young had his own problems. On September 13, he was officially expunged from the Klan. In addition, George Galligan, the local anti-Klan sheriff, got rid of Young's men on the force and made Ora Thomas his special deputy. Thomas was a bootlegger and gangster, and he and Young fiercely hated one another. The two men clashed several times, but their animosity boiled over in January 1925 in a Herrin cigar store.

Thomas walked into the cigar store, located in the European Hotel, with his hand on a pistol that he carried in his coat pocket. In the corner of the room, Young was arguing with a man, and several onlookers watched, absorbed in what was taking place. One of the onlookers glanced toward Thomas and then quickly went out the back door. At that, Young turned around. In an instant, both men had drawn guns and began firing.

When the smoke cleared, four bodies were on the floor, including two of Young's guards. Both Young and Thomas were dying, having shot one another. Both men succumbed to their wounds in pools of blood on the floor of the cigar store.

Not long after, the hold of the Ku Klux Klan over Williamson County was finally broken.

During the years that have become known as the Roaring Twenties, the attention of the entire world often fell on Illinois. Everyone seemed to be painfully aware of the carnage and bloodshed that was taking place in Chicago, but the violence there was hardly more sensational than the gang violence that erupted in the southern part of the state. In fact, the Kefauver Committee, a U.S. Senate committee that investigated organized crime and was chaired by Senator Estes Kefauver of Tennessee, stated that the gang battles in Illinois "reached a peak in bloodiness unparalleled in United States crime history." The focus of the violence in Illinois, the panel pointed out, "was in the coal-mining districts of that state, and the center of the war was in Williamson County, which finally came to be known as 'Bloody' Williamson County."

One of the legends to emerge from the southern Illinois gang wars was Charlie Birger, a swashbuckling bootlegger, gambler, saloonkeeper, and self-styled "do-gooder," who left an indelible mark on the bloody history of the region. He lived hard, died early, and became the last man to hang on the gallows in the state of Illinois.

Charlie Birger was born of Jewish Russian immigrants sometime between 1880 and 1883. He was raised in St. Louis and in Glen Carbon, Illinois. In 1901, he joined the 13th U.S. Cavalry and served in the Spanish-American War. Afterward, he worked as a cowboy in the West and then drifted back to East St. Louis. Here he made friends who would eventually go on to become his bitter enemies and deadly foes in the Prohibition gang wars. These friends were the Shelton brothers, Carl, Earl, and Bernie, and with Birger, they would battle the powerful Ku Klux Klan.

The Shelton brothers were an integral part of the violence in the region. As friends, and later foes, of Charlie Birger, the Sheltons took part in what can only be considered an all-out war between the bootlegger factions. In fact, their attack on Birger's Shady Rest roadhouse is still considered the only time that bombs have been dropped during aerial warfare in America. It should probably be mentioned, though, that the bombs were so badly constructed that they never exploded.

The Shelton boys grew up in southern Illinois. Their father had moved to Wayne County from Kentucky, married a local girl, and started farming. The boys were brought up on the farm but from early youth showed an aversion to hard work. As they got older, Carl and Earl began leaving home for months at a time to drive taxicabs in St. Louis and East St. Louis. When he was old enough, Bernie joined them. The boys quickly sought out trouble, and all of them were soon mixed up with the law.

In the fall of 1915, Earl was convicted of armed robbery and sentenced to eighteen and a half months at the Illinois State Penitentiary at Pontiac. About the same time, Carl was arrested in St. Louis and charged with petty larceny. He was sentenced to a year in a workhouse. Bernie was arrested in a stolen car while Earl was still in prison. He was also sentenced to a year in the workhouse but was paroled.

After Carl and Earl served out their sentences, both of them went to work in the Illinois coal mines, but around 1920, they moved back to East St. Louis, where Bernie was now living. They went into the bootlegging and gambling business and opened illegal joints in East St. Louis and the surrounding area. Soon the Sheltons were in command of a large portion of southern Illinois.

During the Klan wars in Williamson County, the Sheltons threw in with Charlie Birger to oppose the authority of S. Glenn Young. Once those problems were over, the two rival operations began fighting one another—leading to more bloodshed and murder than Illinois had ever seen.

In the early 1920s, Birger moved to Harrisburg. By this time, he was married to his second wife, had two children, and was a successful "businessman." He had started a number of profitable speakeasies and brothels that offered not only liquor and prostitutes, but gambling as well. Most of the establishments were located in and around Harrisburg. Birger also earned a reputation, both good and bad. On one hand, he called himself the "protector of Harrisburg" and helped many people who were in need. On the other hand, in 1923, he was said to have killed two men in a span of three days. Birger claimed self-defense for the first killing and was cleared of all charges. He was wounded in the second and spent time in the Herrin Hospital after a stray bullet struck his lung. Other murders followed, and before his death, he readily admitted that he had killed men, "but never a good one."

In December 1923, Birger was arrested during one of the early bootlegging raids organized by S. Glenn Young. Once Birger got out of jail, he began building what would become his most prominent establishment, Shady Rest. It was located about halfway between Marion and Harrisburg on Route 13, and the roadhouse drew disreputable characters and customers from all over the region. It would become the base of Birger's illegal operations.

At about this same time, Birger joined forced with the Shelton brothers. At the time they joined up with Birger, the Sheltons were running bootleg liquor from Florida for distribution in southern Illinois. Birger allowed the Sheltons to use Harrisburg as a layover and shipping point, and they also worked together to establish slot machines and gambling across the region.

Shady Rest opened for business in 1924, offering bootleg liquor, gambling, cockfights, and dogfights. Although it was notorious all over southern Illinois, no police officials ever raided or bothered the place. It was no secret what it was being used for or that it had been built to withstand a siege if necessary. It had been constructed with foot-thick log walls and a deep basement. Rifles, submachine guns, and boxes of ammunition were stored inside, along with canned food and water. Floodlights, supplied with electricity that was generated on the grounds, prevented anyone from sneaking up on Shady Rest in the night.

The place became very popular with the locals until early 1926, when the relationship between Birger and the Sheltons fell apart. After that, the bloody climate of the location kept many customers away. Regardless, a number of people in the area still chose to see Charlie Birger as a public benefactor rather than a killer and bootlegger. Accounts have it that Birger once gave coal to all of the destitute families in Harrisburg during one bitterly cold winter. He also provided schoolbooks for children who couldn't afford them and vowed that he would not let Harrisburg residents play at his gambling tables.

Why the bloody rift developed between Birger and the Sheltons is unclear. Most likely, it was simply business that became personal. The two groups had originally united to fight back against Young and the Klan's encroachment on their business. Once the Klan was wiped out, there was no one left to fight but each other. Regardless of why it started, though, it plunged southern Illinois into chaos. The war began in 1926, and small towns and roadhouses in the region were terrorized as both sides built armed vehicles to carry out deadly reprisals against one another. Machine guns blasted, speakeasies were torn apart with gunfire, and many people died during the fighting.

In November 1926, a Birger associate named John Milroy was gunned down as he left a roadhouse in the town of Colp. The mayor and the chief of police, called in from another roadhouse nearby, were shot at from the darkness as they got out of their car. The mayor was fatally wounded, but the police chief managed to escape with a shattered hand. Both men were enemies of the Sheltons.

A few days later, a homemade bomb was tossed from a speeding car toward Shady Rest. The bomb had been intended for the building, but it missed, and Birger's hideout was unharmed. Two days later, machine gunners allegedly sent by Birger shot up the home of Joe Adams, the mayor of West City. He was a friend of the Sheltons and a mechanic who often did work on the armored vehicle they had built.

Then, hours later, the only bombs ever dropped during aerial warfare in America fell on Shady Rest. In full daylight, an airplane flew low over Birger's hideout. A few bundles were thrown from the cockpit, which turned out to be dynamite bound around bottles of nitroglycerin. The "bombs" were so poorly constructed that they never exploded. The following week, a more effective bomb was thrown in response, this time by the Birger gang. It exploded in front of Joe Adams's house, damaging the front porch, blowing the door off its hinges, and shattering the windows.

On December 12, two men came to the door of the mayor's house and told his wife they had a letter from Carl Shelton. When he answered his wife's call, one of the men handed Adams a note. While he read it, both of them pulled guns from their coats and shot the man in the chest. He lived just long enough to tell his wife that he hadn't recognized the killers. She blamed the killing on Charlie Birger.

The gang war soon reached its climax. Around midnight on January 9, 1927, a farmer who lived a short distance from Shady Rest was awakened by five or six gunshots. They were followed by a massive explosion that destroyed Shady Rest and shook the farmer's home. The fire burned so hot that no one dared approach the ruined structure until morning. By then it was merely ashes and burned embers. Among the remains were four bodies, charred beyond recognition. One of the corpses later turned out to be that of Elmo Thomasson, a member of the Birger gang.

From all appearances, Birger was finished, but he still managed to beat the Sheltons in the end. Although he had failed to best his rivals with guns and dynamite, he did manage to beat them by using the U.S. government against them instead. Back in 1925, a post office messenger in Collinsville had been robbed of a mine payroll adding up to around $21,000. The crime had remained unsolved. Birger contacted the postal inspector and managed to convince him that the Sheltons had pulled the job. A federal grand jury indicted the brothers, and the courts convicted them. The Sheltons each were given twenty-five years in federal prison, but they were later awarded new trials.

Once the dust settled, the Sheltons left the area and never returned. They moved their operations to East St. Louis, continuing with bootlegging, prostitution, and gambling. They remained there until driven out, making room for Mafia organizers to turn the city into a major gambling spot. The Sheltons then moved north to Peoria, which they found to be much more hospitable. During the late 1930s, they established themselves and began an operation that comprised most of the illegal rackets in downstate Illinois. Apparently immune to prosecution, they were able to protect themselves from the long arm of the law. There was nothing they could do, however, to protect themselves from other gangsters.

Carl, who had left Peoria to retire to his Wayne County farm, was killed there in the fall of 1947. Earl survived a murderous attack in Fairfield. Roy, a fourth brother, and the oldest, was killed in June 1950 while driving a tractor on Earl's farm. Although he had a criminal record, he had never been associated with Carl, Earl, and Bernie. None of the Shelton murders were ever solved.

Bernie Shelton survived until 1948. He was killed on the morning of July 26, when he was shot to death by an assassin who was hiding on a hill near the tavern that he owned. As Bernie walked toward his automobile, a bullet slammed into his body, and he crumpled to the ground. He died a short time later. His life ended violently, the same way he had lived it.

Charlie Birger technically had won the war for southern Illinois, and he had put his rivals out of business in the region, but his victory wouldn't last. Things started to go bad when the police arrested another Birger associate, Harry Thomasson, on a robbery charge.

Franklin County state's attorney Roy Martin suspected that the man also was involved in the murder of West City's mayor, Joe Adams. Thomasson's relationship with Birger had been rocky since the burning of Shady Rest. Harry had begun to suspect that Birger himself had been responsible for the bombing of the roadhouse, which had killed his brother, Elmo. Looking for a deal, he confessed to the murder of Joe Adams and implicated Birger in the crime. He explained that Charlie had paid him $150 to do it.

This was the beginning of the end. Another Birger gang member, Art Newman, who had once owned the Arlington Hotel in East St. Louis, had fled to California but was captured there and brought back to Illinois on a murder charge. On the trip back, he confessed to taking part in the murder of Lory Price, a state patrol officer who had been a friend of Birger's. Witnesses had indicated that Price had been at Shady Rest on the night of the explosion and that he and his wife had disappeared mysteriously a short time later. Newman was indicted for the murder, along with Birger and four other gang members. Price's body was found in a field by a farmer, and his wife's corpse was later discovered in an old mine shaft near Johnston City.

Birger was arrested for the murder of Joe Adams on April 29, 1927, and was tried that summer in Franklin County. In late July, after twenty-four hours of deliberation, the jury returned with its verdict, finding Birger guilty. He was sentenced to death, although he was granted a stay of execution as he appealed the verdict. In late February 1928, the Illinois Supreme Court denied his appeal and sentenced him to die on April 13. Birger claimed to be relieved and said that he would "rather die than spend another ten months in jail."

He attempted another appeal, but it was turned down on April 12 by the State Board of Pardons and Paroles. After this failure, Birger's lawyer rushed to Benton and filed another petition. This one was in the name of Charlie's nephew Nathan Birger, and it asked for a sanity hearing. The execution was postponed again, and on April 16, the hearing began. Birger made a desperate attempt to escape death, making a fool of himself by cursing at reporters, cowering, and rolling his head from side to side. Spectators in the crowd actually laughed at him, and the jury took just twelve minutes to find him totally sane. He was now scheduled to die on April 19. He would be the last man to die on the gallows in the state of Illinois. During that same month, the Illinois legislature abolished hanging and substituted the electric chair as a more humane method of execution in the state.

Thanks to Charlie's notoriety, the town of Benton was characterized as having a "county fair atmosphere" on the day of the hanging. Thousands of people jammed the streets, although only a few hundred of them actually had tickets to the execution. Birger climbed the steps of the scaffold with a bright smile on his face, laughing and joking with the officials. "It's a beautiful world," he said with a grin, and those were the last words of the man who had become a larger-than-life Illinois character. Six minutes later, Charlie Birger was dead.

A chapter in southern Illinois' colorful history had come to an end.

CHAPTER 4
The Starved Rock Murders

The land around legendary Starved Rock State Park, near Utica, is a place of great history and intense tragedy. It is one of the most beautiful natural areas in the state, yet it has seen more than its share of death and tragedy over the years, dating back to Indian massacres that occurred more than 300 years ago and continuing into the modern era.

In 1960, the violence of the past returned to Starved Rock with the discovery of the bludgeoned bodies of three women from Riverside on March 14. The women's bloody corpses were found in one of the park's fabulous box canyons. The murders sent the entire Illinois River Valley into a panic.

The three middle-aged women, Mildred Lindquist, Lillian Oetting, and Frances Murphy, had arrived for a four-day holiday at Starved Rock. The three friends, who all attended the Riverside Presbyterian Church, had been eager for an outing together. Mrs.

Oetting, who had spent the entire winter nursing her husband after a heart attack, was especially looking forward to several days of hiking, bird-watching, and spending time outdoors. Employees at the park's lodge later recalled the arrival of the three ladies. Frances Murphy parked her gray station wagon in the inn's parking area, and she and her friends unloaded their few pieces of luggage. They registered for two rooms, dropped off their bags, and then ate lunch in the dining room. Afterward, they left on a hike, carrying a camera and a small pair of binoculars.

The women walked away from the lodge and followed trails that eventually led to the dead end of St. Louis Canyon, where steep, rocky walls framed a majestic, frozen waterfall. The three women were only one mile from the lodge. They took several photographs of the scenic canyon and then turned to leave. Moments later, the women's final, horrifying moments began.

Later that night, George Oetting tried to telephone his wife at the lodge. She had promised to call him, but when she had not, Oetting placed his own call. He was told by staff on duty at the desk that his wife was not available. It was surmised that the ladies had gone out somewhere, and the staff member suggested that she would call in the morning. Unconcerned, Oetting went to bed.

On Tuesday morning, he called the lodge again and once more asked to speak to his wife. The employee who answered mistakenly told the worried man that the three women had been seen at breakfast and were simply out of the lodge at that time. Reassured, Oetting ended the call.

That night, a late-winter storm hit the Illinois Valley. In St. Louis Canyon, several inches of snow covered up footprints, bloodstains, and other vital pieces of evidence around three cold and still bodies. The near-blizzard conditions continued all night long, making the roads in the park nearly impassable.

George Oetting telephoned the lodge again on Wednesday morning, but his wife and her friends still could not be located. At his insistence, employees entered the women's rooms and found that their beds and bags were untouched. A quick check of the parking lot also showed that the Murphy station wagon had not been moved. Shocked, Oetting realized that his wife and her friends had now been missing for more than forty hours.

As soon as Oetting broke off the call, he telephoned his long-time friend Virgil W. Peterson, the operating director of the Chicago Crime Commission. When Peterson learned of the news, he contacted the state police and other law enforcement agencies in the area. Within minutes, word of the missing women had reached the LaSalle County Sheriff's Office, and Sheriff Ray Eutsey began organizing search parties to look for the missing women.

A short time later, a local news reporter, Bill Danley, heard from several young boys that they had found bodies on one of the park trails. Recognizing the boys, he called the Starved Rock Lodge, where law enforcement officials had gathered, and then the newspaper to report the discovery. In a matter of minutes, the story was flashing across news wires around the country.

Danley was among those who entered St. Louis Canyon and got the first look at the bodies. The three mutilated women were lying side by side, partially covered with snow. They were on their backs under a small ledge, with their lower clothing torn away and their legs spread open. Each of them had been beaten viciously about the head, and two of the bodies were tied together with heavy white twine. They were covered with blood, and their exposed legs were blackened with bruises.

State police detectives soon arrived and began a search of the immediate area. Except for the floor of the overhang where the bodies were found, the entire canyon was covered in nearly six inches of snow. The fine, white powder had to be carefully removed, and as it was, signs of a violent struggle were revealed. Mrs. Murphy's camera was found about ten feet from the victims, its leather case smeared with blood and its strap broken. The party also found the women's bloody binoculars. A short distance away, LaSalle County state's attorney Harland Warren stumbled across a frozen tree limb that was streaked with blood. The snow beneath it was covered with blood, and he and the others realized that this was likely the murder weapon. A trail of gore also led them to speculate that the women had been killed deeper in the canyon, and then their bodies had been dragged and positioned under the rock ledge. The bodies remained in place for hours, until pathologists and state crime lab officials could arrive. The vigil lasted long into the night, and then, by the light of lanterns and flashlights, the victims were removed on cloth stretchers.

The bodies were taken to the Hulse Funeral Home in Ottawa, where they were examined and autopsied. The women had obviously been molested, but because of the cold and the limitations of medical techniques at the time, the doctors failed to find any evidence of rape. They were able to determine the time of death, however, placing it shortly after the women had enjoyed lunch at the lodge. No motive was suggested for the murders, but robbery was dismissed, as the women had left their money and jewelry behind in the rooms when they went for their afternoon hike.

The investigation almost immediately stalled. There were few clues to follow, and theories began to grow wilder and wilder. Things were further confused by all of those who wanted to maintain jurisdiction in the case. The state's attorney, a hard-working and respected official, was technically in charge, but the state police maintained their authority in the case because the murders were committed on park property. The first major dispute between Warren and state police officials arose over the theory that the murders had been committed by Chicago gangsters. State investigators suggested that professional killers might have committed the murders in an effort to get even with Chicago Crime Commissioner Virgil Peterson, a close friend of the families of all three victims. Warren immediately dismissed this idea, as he had a hard time believing that mob killers would travel 100 miles to commit three murders and not bring a weapon along. The two law enforcement camps clashed, but Warren was in a bind. He was forced to deal with the state authorities because the officials in LaSalle County simply had no experience dealing with crimes of this nature.

The investigation became one of plodding police work. State officers began intensely questioning the nearly fifty men and women who were either employees or guests at the park during the days when the murders took place. All were subjected to polygraph tests, and every one of them passed. During this time, detectives were going over the crime scene again, looking for more clues, but they were finding nothing.

As the investigation slowly moved forward, fear was gripping the region. Newspapers and radio broadcasters around the state widely reported the slow progress of the investigation and elevated the level of panic in the area. The number of overnight guests at the Starved Rock Lodge dropped off to almost nothing. Reporters from wire services, television stations, and national magazines soon replaced the late-winter guests at the lodge, and competition for daily stories became fierce. Since little was happening in the case, bold headlines were made out of the most basic of police news releases. Lodge employees later recalled, with sardonic humor, watching the big-city reporters grab up copies of the local newspaper when it was delivered. Then, with this small-town paper in hand, they would file their own stories over the telephone with their editors.

The continued newspaper scrutiny of the case kept pressure on police officials to make progress, especially at Harland Warren's county office. He was doing everything in his power to move the investigation forward, but he had a hard time coping with the pressure. Money was becoming a problem as well, since the investigation budget was soaring. The county board was deluged with requests for funds from Warren's office and from state officers. The board felt that the state should pay for the investigation, because the crimes had been committed on state property, so a special session of the board was called. The session ended in a shouting match between supervisors and members of the board. Warren's office and the state officers were loudly criticized, and news reporters were stunned to see the lack of cooperation. Editorials soon appeared that drew attention to the problems, and the special session ended up having a positive result. Confidence was soon restored in the investigation, and it began to move ahead. Unfortunately, though, a scandal over professional blunders soon destroyed that confidence.

The problem began when a routine check of personal items found on the victims revealed that a small diamond ring was missing from Mrs. Oetting's effects. Going after what they thought was an important lead, detectives began visiting and sending out notices to Illinois pawnshops in a frantic search for the ring. Hundreds of man-hours were spent on the search over the course of the next month, and then finally the state crime lab in Springfield announced that they had found the ring—inside Mrs. Oetting's bloody glove. It apparently had slipped off her hand when her clothing was being removed. Precious time and money had been spent pursuing this false lead, and journalists publicized the blunder with glee, blaming detectives and lab workers by name. The superintendent of the crime lab, James Christensen, defended his overworked staff, but eventually, despite years of exemplary service, he resigned from his position. County authorities, fearing that other mistakes might have been made, quietly sent all of the physical evidence they had to the crime lab for the state of Michigan for reexamination.

The summer of 1960 was brutal for state's attorney Harland Warren, who was under ever-increasing pressure to solve the murders. He decided to pursue an independent investigation and see what progress could be made. Using his own money, Warren purchased a microscope and began intently conducting a study of the twine the killer had left at the crime scene. Research revealed that two kinds of twine had been used: a twenty-ply cord and a twelve-ply one. With this information in hand, Warren sought help to follow the lead. Instead of choosing someone from his staff, he handpicked two county detectives who would report to him alone: Deputies Bill Dummett and Wayne Hess. Both men were trustworthy and intelligent and would not leak the details of what Warren was doing to the newspapers.

The men started the search for the source of the twine at the most logical place—Starved Rock Lodge. In September 1960, Warren and his deputies met with the manager of the lodge's kitchen. Within minutes, and without much difficulty, Warren found both kinds of twine, which were each used for wrapping food. Dummett and Hess soon tracked down the twine's manufacturer in the lodge's purchasing records. The twine used to bind the murder victims had been taken, without question, from the supply in the lodge's kitchen. Just as Warren had always suspected, the killer either worked at or had access to the park's lodge.

Even though the lodge workers had already passed polygraph tests, Warren decided to run them again, using his own expert. Hiring a specialist who worked for a prominent Chicago firm, Warren recalled all of the employees who had worked during the week of the murder. One by one, they were taken to a small cabin located near the lodge for another exam. The first dozen or so were quickly cleared, and Warren and the deputies wondered if they might be wasting their time. Then Bill Dummett brought in a former dishwasher named Chester Otto Weger, and everything changed.

When Weger's polygraph test was completed, Warren noticed that the examiner's face had gone pale. As soon as Weger left the cabin, the technician ended months of countless leads and wasted time. He turned to Warren and the two deputies and quietly stated: "That's your man."

Weger, age twenty-one, was a slight, small man with a wife and two young children. He had worked at the park until that summer, when he resigned to go into business with his father as a house painter. Warren intensified the investigation of the man, and strangely, Weger happily cooperated with him. He surrendered a piece of a buckskin jacket that he owned so that some suspicious dark stains on it could be examined. It turned out to be human blood, but in 1960, it could not be typed and matched to a specific victim. Warren also asked the suspect to submit to further polygraph tests, and again Weger agreed. He was given an entire series of tests, and he failed all of them.

Once the jacket was determined to be stained with blood, Warren put the former dishwasher under constant surveillance by the state police. Warren, along with Dummett and Hess, began checking into Weger's past and also into similar crimes in the area that might have escalated into murder. Dummett came across a reported rape and robbery case that had taken place about a mile from Starved Rock in 1959. With Warren's approval, he approached the young female victim with a stack of mug shots. As she slowly sorted through them, she began to scream as she came across the face of Chester Weger.

With this positive identification, Warren could easily have ordered Weger arrested, but he was forced to wait. A new problem had reared its ugly head. With all the time and energy involved in the investigation, Warren had worked very little on his campaign for reelection. If he booked Weger on rape and murder charges before the election, defense attorneys would simply say that he had done so as a stunt to retain his job. He left Weger under surveillance but put his arrest on the back burner so that he would not jeopardize the case with the election. Confident of his record of cleaning gambling and prostitution out of LaSalle County during his eight years in office, Warren let his past actions speak for themselves. Unfortunately, his opponent let the "bungling" of the Starved Rock murder case speak for him. Out of 60,000 votes cast in the election, Warren lost by nearly 3,500.

Disappointed by the election results, Warren still had time in office to pursue the case against Weger. Although his evidence was not as strong as he would have liked, he obtained an arrest warrant against Weger for the 1959 rape and ordered Hess and Dummett to pick him up. Warren believed that when Weger saw all the evidence mounting against him, he would confess to the crime—and the Starved Rock murders.

Warren made careful plans with his two deputies about how to interrogate Weger before confronting him with murder charges. A short time later, Hess and Dummett arrived at the young man's apartment and explained that they had some more questions for him. They made no mention of the arrest warrants that were waiting at the courthouse. Once they had him in custody, the officers began to question him about the rape and also began to press him about the murders. They kept him in the interrogation room until past midnight, and then finally, weary of questions and nearly exhausted, Weger stopped in midsentence and asked to see his family. A police car was dispatched to his parents' home in Oglesby, and his mother and father were brought to the courthouse. Dummett and Hess gave them a few minutes alone with their son.

In his official statement, taken the next day, Deputy Hess stated: "When Bill stepped out of the back room in the state's attorney's office to show Mr. and Mrs. Weger to the door so they could go home, I could see that something was bothering Chester. I said, 'Chester, why don't you tell me about it? There are just the two of us here . . . just tell me about it.' He said, 'All right. I did it. I got scared. I tried to grab their pocketbook, they fought and I hit them.' The pocketbook that Weger claimed he had tried to take was actually Mrs. Murphy's camera.

Minutes later, a court reporter was summoned, and the confession was transcribed and signed by Weger. During the confession, when he was asked why he had dragged the bodies under the overhang in St. Louis Canyon, Weger said that he had spotted a small airplane flying low over the park. He said he was afraid it was a state police plane, so he moved the bodies so that they could not be seen from above. A few days later, the flight over the park was confirmed by the pilot's testimony and logbook.

Weger confessed several more times to the murders over the next few days and even reenacted the murders for a crowd of policemen and reporters at the canyon. But then, after his first meeting with his court-appointed attorney, Weger changed his story and stated that he was innocent of all the charges. He claimed that Dummett and Hess had coerced a confession from him by threatening him with a gun. Weger also said that Dummett had fed him the information about the airplane. He claimed to have been in Oglesby at the time of the killings.

Weger was brought to trial. Selection of the jury took almost two weeks, and the trial began on January 20, 1961. The new state's attorney, Robert E. Richardson, was in charge of the prosecution, assisted by Anthony Raccuglia. The trial had gained national attention, and because the two prosecutors had never tried a murder case before, the judge suggested that Harland Warren be named as a special prosecutor for this case only. Richardson, who had strongly criticized Warren during the election, dismissed the idea. Richardson and Raccuglia decided to file charges against Weger for only one of the three murders. That way, if they failed to convict him, he still could be tried for the other two. They sought the death penalty in the case.

On March 4, the jury brought back a guilty verdict for Chester Weger, and he was sentenced to life in prison. He was incarcerated at the Statesville Penitentiary in Joliet and remains in prison today at the Illinois River Correctional Center in Canton. Weger has been denied parole two dozen times since 1972, and most feel that he belongs securely behind bars.

In the minds of some people, however, there are questions about the case that remain unanswered. Many feel that the evidence that was used to convict Weger would not stand up in court today. Others question how a small, slight man like Weger could have overpowered the three middle-aged women, and then moved their bodies by himself to hide under the rock overhang.

Others who believe in Weger's innocence point to a deathbed confession that allegedly occurred in 1982 or 1983. A Chicago police sergeant named Mark Gibson submitted an affidavit in 2006 that recounted the confession, which was being used in court to support a motion for new DNA tests in the Starved Rock murder case. In the affidavit, Gibson stated that he and his partner, now deceased, were called to Rush-St. Luke's Presbyterian Hospital to see a terminally ill patient who wanted to "clear her conscience."

The affidavit stated: "The woman was lying in a hospital bed. I went over toward her, and she grabbed hold of my hand. She indicated that when she was younger, she had been with her friends at a state park when something happened." The woman then told Gibson that she was at a park in Utica, and things "got out of hand," multiple victims were killed, and "they dragged the bodies."

Gibson said that the woman's daughters cut the interview short, shouting that their mother was out of her mind and ordering the police from the room. In the affidavit, Gibson did not provide the exact date of the interview or the woman's name, but said he had passed the information along to a detective. The affidavit did not address whether there had been any follow-up or why the confession was not presented until 2006. The alleged confession was not allowed into the court hearings, although new DNA tests were ordered. They failed to clear Weger of anything, however, because the samples had been corrupted over the years.

After these attempts for release failed, a clemency petition was sent to Governor Rod Blagojevich, but it was denied in June 2007.

To this day, Chester Weger continues to maintain that he was framed for the murders by Deputies Dummett and Hess. But both deputies, until the day each of them died, insisted that Weger had confessed. They firmly believed that he had committed the murders and had been the perpetrator of one of the most heinous acts in the bloody history of Starved Rock.

CHAPTER 5
H. H. Holmes and the Murder Castle

In 1893, Chicago was host to a spectacular World's Fair—the Columbian Exposition—which celebrated the anniversary of Columbus's discovery of America. It was a boom time for the city, and thousands of people came from all over the country to attend. Unfortunately, though, at the end of the fair, the list of those gone missing was extensive, and as the police later tried to track down the whereabouts of these people, the trail often turned cold on the South Side of Chicago. Everything was not as shiny and beautiful as the advertising for the Exposition's "White City" would have everyone believe, for a "devil" who became known as America's first real serial killer was alive and well on the city's South Side, luring visitors to his "hotel," where scores of them vanished without a trace—never to be seen again.

Herman Mudgett, who went by the name H. H. Holmes, was born in 1860 in Gilmanton, New Hampshire, where his father was a wealthy and respected citizen and the local postmaster for nearly twenty-five years. In 1878, Holmes married Clara Lovering, and that same year, he began studying medicine at a small college in Burlington, Vermont. He paid his tuition with a tidy legacy that his wife had inherited. Even as a student, though, Holmes began to dabble in crime. Using cadavers stolen from the morgue, he would stage accidents in which the corpses appeared to have died so that he could collect on insurance policies he had taken out. Eventually Holmes dropped out of sight, soon abandoning his wife and infant. Clara returned to New Hampshire and never saw her husband again.

In 1885, Holmes turned up in Chicago and opened an office in the North Shore suburb of Wilmette. Holmes had filed for—but never went through with—divorce from Clara Lovering, but this did not stop him from marrying another woman, Myrtle Z. Belknap, whose father, John Belknap, was a wealthy businessman in Wilmette. Although the marriage produced a daughter, Myrtle remained living in Wilmette while Holmes began living in Chicago. Myrtle ended the marriage in 1889.

Shortly after Holmes married Myrtle, he opened another office, this time in downtown Chicago, selling the A.B.C. Copier, a machine for copying documents. He operated from an office on South Dearborn, but the copier was a failure and he vanished again, leaving his creditors with $9,000 in worthless notes.

In 1887, Holmes took over the management of a drugstore in Englewood, on the south side of the city. The owner of the store soon conveniently vanished, and Holmes later told the curious that she had left town and had sold him the business. She had left no forwarding address.

Holmes acquired a large lot across the street from the drugstore and began construction on an enormous edifice that he planned to operate as a hotel for the upcoming Columbian Exposition in 1893. The purchase of the property was financed by an insurance swindle that was aided by an accomplice named Benjamin Pietzel. There are no records to say what Holmes decided to call this building, but for generations of police officers, crime enthusiasts, and unnerved residents of Englewood, it was known simply by one name—the "Murder Castle."

In 1890, Holmes hired L. L. "Ned" Connor of Davenport, Iowa, as a watchmaker and jeweler for his store. The young man arrived in the city in the company of his wife, Julia, and their daughter, Pearl. The family moved into a small apartment above the store, and soon Julia managed to capture the interest of Holmes. He fired his bookkeeper and hired Julia to take the man's place. Not long after, Connor began to suspect that Holmes was having an affair with his wife. He abandoned his family and went to work for another shop downtown. Holmes took out large insurance policies on Julia and Pearl, naming himself as a beneficiary.

Holmes was spending most of his time on the construction of his new building. It was an imposing structure of three stories and a basement, with false battlements and wooden bay windows that were covered with sheet iron. The structure had more than sixty rooms and fifty-one doors that were cut oddly into various walls. Holmes acted as his own architect for the site and personally supervised the numerous construction crews, all of whom were quickly hired and fired. He discharged them with great fury and refused to pay their wages. He paid for few of the materials that went into the building. In addition to the eccentric general design, the house was also fitted with trapdoors, hidden staircases, secret passages, rooms without windows, chutes that led into the basement, and a staircase that opened out over a steep drop to the alley behind the house.

The first floor of the building contained stores and shops, while the upper floors could be used for spacious living quarters. Holmes also had an office on the second floor, but most of the rooms were to be used for guests—guests who checked in but never checked out. Evidence found later showed that Holmes used some of the rooms as asphyxiation chambers, where his victims were suffocated with gas. All of his "prison rooms" were fitted with alarms that buzzed in Holmes's quarters if a captive attempted to escape.

The castle was completed in 1892, and soon after, Holmes announced that he planned to rent out some of the rooms to tourists who would be arriving en masse for the upcoming Columbian Exposition. It is surmised that many of these tourists never returned home after the fair, but no one knows for sure. The list of the missing when the fair closed was a long one, and for most, foul play was suspected. How many of them fell prey to Holmes is a mystery, but no fewer than fifty people who were reported to the police as missing were traced to the place. Here their trails ended.

An advertisement for lodging during the fair was not the only method that Holmes used for procuring victims. A large number of his female victims came through false classified ads that he placed in small-town newspapers, offering jobs to young ladies. When the applicant arrived, and if Holmes was convinced that she had told no one of her destination, she would become his prisoner. Holmes placed newspaper ads for marriage as well, describing himself as a wealthy businessman who was searching for a suitable wife. Those who answered this ad often vanished without a trace.

Amazingly, Holmes was able to keep his murder operation a secret for four years. He slaughtered an unknown number of people, mostly women, in the castle. He later confessed to twenty-eight murders, although the actual number of victims is believed to be much higher. There is no question that Holmes was one of the most prolific and depraved killers in American history.

In 1893, Homes met a young woman named Minnie Williams. He told her that his name was Harry Gordon and that he was a wealthy inventor. Holmes's interest in her had been piqued when he learned that she was the heir to a Texas real estate fortune. She was in Chicago working as an instructor for a private school. It wasn't long before she and Holmes were engaged to be married. This was a turn of events that did not make Julia Connor happy. Not long after the engagement became official, both Julia and Pearl disappeared.

When Ned Connor later inquired after them, Holmes explained that they had moved to Michigan. In his later confession, he admitted that Julia had died during a bungled abortion he had performed on her. He had poisoned Pearl. He later admitted that he murdered the woman and her child because of her jealous feelings toward Minnie Williams. He added: "But I would have gotten rid of her anyway. I was tired of her."

Minnie Williams lived at the Castle for more than a year and knew more about Holmes's crimes than any other person. Besides being ultimately responsible for the deaths of Julia and Pearl Connor, Minnie was also believed to have instigated the murder of Emily Van Tassel, a young lady who lived on Robey Street. Emily was only seventeen and worked at a candy store on the first floor of the castle. There is no indication of what caused her to catch the eye of Holmes, but she vanished just one month after his offer of employment.

Minnie also knew about the murder of Emmeline Cigrand, a beautiful young woman who worked as a stenographer at the Keely Institute in Dwight. Ben Pietzel had gone there to take a drunkenness cure and told Holmes of the girl's beauty when he returned to Chicago. Holmes then contacted her and offered her a large salary to work for him in Chicago. She accepted the job and came to the Castle—but never left it. Holmes later confessed that he had locked the girl in one of his soundproof rooms and raped her. He stated that he killed her because Minnie Williams objected to his lusting after the attractive young woman.

A visit to Chicago by Minnie's sister Nannie may provide more evidence of Minnie's murderous ways and her willingness to go along with Holmes's schemes. In June 1893, Holmes seduced Nannie while she was staying at the Castle and had no trouble persuading her to sign over her share of some property in Fort Worth. She disappeared a month later, and the explanation was that she had gone back to Texas, but according to Holmes, it was Minnie who killed her. When Minnie learned Nannie had been consorting with

Holmes, the two of them got into a heated argument. Minnie hit her sister over the head with a chair, and she died; then Minnie and Holmes dropped the body into Lake Michigan.

A short time later, Holmes and Minnie traveled to Denver in the company of another young woman, Georgianna Yoke, who had come to Chicago from Indiana with a tarnished reputation. On January 17, 1894, Holmes and Georgianna were married at the Vendome Hotel in Denver, with Minnie as their witness. After that, the wedding party, which apparently consisted of the three of them, traveled to Texas, where they claimed Minnie's property and arranged a horse swindle. Holmes purchased several railroad cars of horses with counterfeit banknotes. The horses were then shipped to St. Louis and sold. Holmes made off with a fortune, but it was this swindle that would later destroy him.

The threesome returned to Chicago, and this was the last time Minnie was ever seen alive. Holmes later claimed that Minnie had killed her sister in a fit of passion and then fled to Europe. Her body was never found, but it is believed to have joined those of other victims in the acid vat in the basement.

In July 1894, Holmes was arrested for the first time. It was not for murder, but for one of his schemes: the earlier horse swindle that ended in St. Louis. Georgianna promptly bailed him out, but while in jail, he struck up a conversation with a convicted train robber named Marion Hedgepeth, who was serving a twenty-five-year sentence. Holmes had concocted a plan to bilk an insurance company and offered Hedgepeth a commission in exchange for the name of an attorney who could be trusted. He was directed to Colonel Jeptha Howe, who went along with Holmes's plan of faking his death. When it was all over, the insurance company suspected fraud and refused to pay. Holmes returned to Chicago without pressing the claim and began concocting a new version of the same scheme.

A month later, Holmes, Howe, and Ben Pietzel concocted a new plan. Pietzel was sent to Philadelphia, where Holmes planned to fake his death and put a burned corpse in Pietzel's place. The scheme went off without a hitch, except that instead of substituting a corpse for Pietzel's body, Holmes actually killed him. Within days, attorney Jeptha Howe filed a claim with the insurance company on behalf of Carrie Pietzel and collected the money. He kept $2,500, and Holmes took the remainder. He later gave $500 to Mrs. Pietzel but then took it back, explaining that he would invest it for her.

The only other person who did not get paid was Marion Hedgepeth. Holmes never bothered to contact the train robber again. Hedgepeth brooded over this awhile and then decided to turn Holmes in to the authorities. The police notified the insurance company, which passed on the information to Frank P. Geyer, a Pinkerton agent, who immediately began an investigation. Holmes was eventually arrested in Philadelphia on November 17, 1894.

Holmes was given the choice of being returned to Texas and hanged as a horse thief or confessing to the insurance scheme that had led to the death of Ben Pietzel. He chose insurance fraud, thinking he would be safe, but his entire tapestry of crime was beginning to unravel. Detective Geyer was slowly starting to uncover the dark secrets of H. H. Holmes and began trying to discover the fate of the Pietzel children. Their mother had been found but told police that her children had been in Holmes's care. Holmes swore that Minnie Williams had taken the children with her to London, where she planned to open a massage parlor, but Geyer was sure that he was lying. In June 1895, Holmes entered a guilty plea for a single count of insurance fraud, but Geyer expanded his investigation.

Throughout his questioning, Holmes refused to reveal any explanation of what had become of Carrie Pietzel's three children, Howard, Nellie, and Alice. Fearing the worst, Geyer set out to try to discover their fate—and his worst fears soon were realized. He followed Holmes's trail for eight months through the Midwest and Canada, stopping in each city to investigate the house that Holmes had been renting there. In Toronto, he found the bodies of Nellie and Alice Pietzel buried in the backyard of a cottage, and in the Indianapolis suburb of Irvington, he discovered Howard's charred remains in the stove of a house that Holmes had rented for a week.

As Holmes's crimes came to light, the police began to search his residence in Chicago. None of the officers would ever forget what they found there, and detectives devoted several weeks to searching and making a floor plan of the Castle.

The second floor proved to be a labyrinth of narrow, winding passages with doors that opened to brick walls, hidden stairways, cleverly concealed doors, blind hallways, secret panels, hidden passages, and a clandestine vault that was only big enough for one person to stand in. The room was alleged to be a homemade "gas chamber," equipped with a chute that would carry a body directly into the basement. The investigators suddenly realized the implications of the iron-plated chamber when they found the single scuffed mark of a woman's footprint on the inside of the door.

In addition to all of the bizarre features, the second level also held thirty-five guest rooms. Half of them were fitted as ordinary sleeping chambers. Several of the other rooms had no windows and could be made airtight by closing the doors. Others were lined with sheet iron and asbestos with scorch marks on the walls, fitted with trapdoors that led to smaller rooms beneath, or were equipped with lethal gas jets that could be used to suffocate or burn the unsuspecting occupants.

This floor also contained Holmes's private apartment, consisting of a bedroom, a bath, and two small chambers that were used as offices. The apartment was located at the front of the building, looking out over 63rd Street. In the floor of the bathroom, concealed under a heavy rug, the police found a trapdoor and a stairway that descended to a room about eight feet square. Two doors led off this chamber, one to a stairway that exited out onto the street and the other giving access to the chute that led down to the basement.

The chamber of horrors in the basement stunned the men even further. This subterranean chamber was located seven feet below the rest of the building and extended out under the sidewalk in front.

Here they found Holmes's blood-spattered dissecting table, his gleaming surgical instruments, his macabre laboratory of torture devices, various jars of poison, and even a wooden box that contained a number of female skeletons. A large stove apparently had been used as a crematorium and still contained ash and portions of bone that had not burned in the intense heat. A search of the ashes also revealed a watch that had belonged to Minnie Williams, some buttons from a dress, and several charred tintype photographs.

Buried in the floor, the police found a huge vat of corrosive acid and two quicklime pits, which were capable of devouring an entire body in a matter of hours. A loose pile of lime was also discovered in a small room that had been built into the corner. The naked footprint of a woman was found embedded in the pile.

Less than two weeks after it was vacated by the police, H. H. Holmes's Murder Castle was purchased by a man named A. M. Clark, who planned to open it as a tourist attraction, capitalizing on the sensationalistic press that surrounded the discoveries inside. On August 19, it was ready to admit its first paying customers, but that same night, Clark's get-rich-quick scheme literally went up in smoke.

No one ever found out how the fire got started. Some saw it as an act of divine retribution, as God purged Chicago of Holmes's chamber of horrors. Others suggested that perhaps it had been a resident of Englewood, ashamed of the blemish that the Castle had created on the city's reputation. The police, on the other hand, took another view. They suspected that a confederate of Holmes had torched the place to conceal incriminating evidence that the investigators had overlooked.

Whatever the source of the fire, it made short work of the building. At precisely 12:13 A.M., a night watchman at the Western Indiana Railroad crossing spotted flames coming through the building's roof. Before he could sound the alarm, a series of explosions rocked the building, blowing out the windows of the candy shop on the first floor. By the time the first fire engines arrived, the blaze was nearly out of control. Half an hour later, the roof collapsed, taking down part of the Castle's rear wall. By the time the blaze was extinguished, about an hour and a half after it was first reported, much of the structure had been consumed.

Although the first-floor shops sustained only minimal damage, the two upper stories of the building were completely gutted. The new "murder museum" was a blackened shell, and A. M. Clark was out of business for good. Contrary to many stories, the fire did not destroy the Castle completely. Even though the second and third floors were sealed off, and their windows boarded over, the first floor remained in operation for many years. A sign shop and a bookstore operated there until the building was sold in 1937. The lot was sold and the building was razed in January 1938 to make way for a post office, which still stands at the site today.

The trial of Herman Mudgett, a.k.a. H. H. Holmes, began in Philadelphia just before Halloween 1895. It lasted for only six days, but it was one of the most sensational of the century. On November 30, the judge passed a sentence of death. Holmes's case was appealed to the Pennsylvania Supreme Court, which affirmed the verdict, and the governor refused to intervene. Holmes was scheduled to die on May 7, 1896, just nine days before his thirty-sixth birthday.

By that time the details of the case had been made public, and people were angry, horrified, and fascinated, especially in Chicago, where most of the evil had occurred. Holmes had given a lurid confession of torture and murder, which appeared in newspapers and magazines, providing a litany of depravity that compares with those of the most insane killers of all time. Even if he had embellished his story, the actual evidence of Holmes's crimes ranks him as one of the country's most active murderers.

He remained unrepentant, though, even at the end. Just before his execution, he visited with two Catholic priests in his cell and even took communion with them, although he refused to ask forgiveness for his crimes. He was led from his cell to the gallows, and a black hood was placed over his head. The trapdoor opened beneath him, and Holmes quickly dropped. His head snapped to the side, but his fingers clenched and his feet danced for several minutes afterward, causing many spectators to look away. Although the force of the fall had broken his neck and the rope had pulled so tightly that it embedded in his flesh, his heart continued to beat for nearly fifteen minutes—providing the final excruciating moments to the life of the man that some called the devil incarnate.

CHAPTER 6
The Sausage Vat Murder

The story of Adolph Luetgert has its beginnings in the heart of Chicago's Northwest Side, a place once filled with factories, middle-class homes, and a large immigrant population. The murder of Luetgert's wife, Louisa, has an unusual place in the history of Illinois crime in that it was one of the only murders ever to drastically affect the sale of a certain kind of food.

Adolph Luetgert was born in Germany and came to America after the Civil War. He lived for a time in Quincy, and in 1872 he came to Chicago, where he pursued several trades, including farming, leather tanning, and eventually starting a wholesale liquor business near Dominick Street. He later turned to sausagemaking, where he found his most lucrative business. After finding out that his German-style sausages were quite popular in Chicago, he built a sausage plant in 1894 at the southwest corner of Hermitage and Diversey. It was here

67

that the massive German would achieve his greatest success—and earn his continued infamy.

Although the hard-working Luetgert soon began to put together a considerable fortune, he was an unhappy and restless man. Luetgert had married his first wife, Caroline Rabaker, in 1872. She gave birth to two boys, only one of whom survived childhood. Caroline died five years later, in November 1877. Luetgert sold his liquor business in 1879 and moved to North and Clybourn Avenues, where he started his first sausage packing plant in the same building he used as a residence. Two months after Caroline's death, Luetgert married an attractive younger woman. This did little to ease his restlessness, however, and he was rumored to be engaged in several affairs during the time when he built a three-story frame house next door to the sausage factory. He resided there with his son and new wife.

His wife, Louisa Bicknese Luetgert, was a beautiful young woman who was ten years younger than her husband. She was a former servant from the Fox River Valley who had met her new husband by chance. He was immediately taken with her, entranced by her diminutive stature and tiny frame. She was less than five feet tall and looked almost childlike next to her burly husband. As a wedding gift, he gave her a unique heavy gold ring with her initials inscribed inside it. He had no idea at the time that this ring would later be his undoing.

After less than three years in the sausage business, Luetgert's finances began to fail. Even though his factory turned out large quantities of sausages, Luetgert found that he could not meet his suppliers' costs. Instead of trying to reorganize his finances, though, he and his business advisor, William Charles, made plans to expand. They attempted to secure more capital to enlarge the factory, but by April 1897, everything had fallen apart. Deep in depression, Luetgert sought solace with his various mistresses, and his excesses and business losses began taking a terrible toll on his marriage. Neighbors frequently heard him and Louisa arguing, and their disagreements became so heated that Luetgert eventually moved his bedroom from the house to a small chamber inside the factory. Soon after, Louisa found out that her husband was having an affair with the family's maid, Mary Simerling, who also happened to be Louisa's niece. She was enraged over this, and this new scandal got the attention of the people in the neighborhood, who were already gossiping about the couple's marital woes.

Luetgert soon gave the neighbors even more to gossip about. One night, during another shouting match with Louisa, he responded to her indignation over his affair with Mary by taking his wife by the throat and choking her. Before she collapsed, Luetgert saw neighbors peering in at him through the parlor window of their home, and he released her. A few days later, Luetgert was seen chasing his wife down the street, shouting at her and waving a revolver. After a couple blocks, Luetgert broke off the chase and walked silently back to the factory.

Then, on May 1, 1897, Louisa disappeared. When questioned about it, Luetgert stated that Louisa had left the previous evening to visit her sister. After several days, though, she did not come back. Soon after, Diedrich Bicknese, Louisa's brother, came to Chicago and called on his sister. He was informed that she was not at home. He came back later, and finding Luetgert at home, he demanded to know where Louisa was. Luetgert calmly told him that Louisa had disappeared on May 1 and never returned. When Diedrich asked why Luetgert had not informed the police about Louisa's disappearance, the sausagemaker simply told him that he was trying to avoid a scandal but had paid two detectives $5 to try to find her.

Diedrich immediately began searching for his sister. He went to Kankakee, thinking that perhaps she might be visiting friends there, but found no one who had seen her. Then he returned to Chicago, and when he found that Louisa still had not come home, now having abandoned her children for days, he went to the police and spoke with Captain Herman Schuettler.

The detective and his men began to search for Louisa. They questioned neighbors and relatives and heard many recitations about the couple's violent arguments. Captain Schuettler was familiar with Luetgert and had had dealings with him in the past. He summoned the sausagemaker to the precinct house on two occasions and each time pressed him about his wife. Schuettler recalled a time when the Luetgerts had lost a family dog, an event that prompted several calls from Luetgert, but noted that when his wife had gone missing, Luetgert had never contacted him. Luetgert again used the excuse that as a "prominent businessman," he could not afford the disgrace and scandal.

The police began searching the alleyways and dragging the rivers, but they also went to the sausage factory and began questioning the employees. One of them, Wilhelm Fulpeck, recalled seeing Louisa around the factory at about 10:30 P.M. on May 1. A young German girl named Emma Schiemicke passed by the factory with her sister at about the same time that evening and remembered seeing Luetgert leading his wife up the alleyway behind the factory.

Frank Bialk, a night watchman at the plant, confirmed both stories. He also had witnessed Luetgert and Louisa at the plant that night. He got only a glimpse of Louisa but saw his employer several times. Shortly after the couple had entered the factory, Luetgert came back outside and gave Bialk a dollar, asking him to get him a bottle of celery compound from a nearby drugstore. When the watchman returned with the medicine, he was surprised to find that the door leading into the main factory was locked. Luetgert appeared and took the medicine. He made no comment about the locked door and sent Bialk back to the engine room.

A little while later, Luetgert again approached the watchman and sent him back to the drugstore to buy a bottle of medicinal spring water. While the watchman was away running errands, Luetgert apparently had been working alone in the factory basement. He had turned on the steam under the middle vat a little before 9 P.M., and it was still running when Bialk returned. The watchman reported that Luetgert had remained in the basement until about 2 A.M.

Bialk found him fully dressed in his office the next day. He asked whether the fires under the vat should be put out, and Luetgert told him to leave them burning, which was odd, since the factory had been closed for several weeks during Luetgert's financial reorganization. Bialk did as he was told, though, and went down to the basement. There he saw a hose sending water into the middle vat, and on the floor in front of it was a sticky, gluelike substance. Bialk noticed that it seemed to contain bits of bone, but he thought nothing of it. Luetgert used all sorts of waste meats to make his sausage, and he assumed that was all it was.

On May 3, another employee, Frank Odorowsky, known as "Smokehouse Frank," also noticed the slimy substance on the factory floor. He feared that someone had boiled something in the factory without Luetgert's knowledge, so he went to his employer to report it. Luetgert told him not to mention the brown slime. As long as he kept silent, Luetgert said, he would have a good job for the rest of his life. Frank went to work scraping the slime off the floor and poured it into a nearby drain that led to the sewer. The larger chunks of waste were placed in a barrel, and Luetgert told him to take the barrel out to the railroad tracks and scatter the contents there.

Following these interviews, Schuettler made another disturbing and suspicious discovery. A short time before Louisa's disappearance, even though the factory had been closed during the reorganization, Luetgert had ordered 325 pounds of crude potash and 50 pounds of arsenic from Lor Owen and Company, a wholesale drug firm. It was delivered to the factory the next day. Another interview with Frank Odorowsky revealed what had happened to the chemicals. On April 24, Luetgert had asked Smokehouse Frank to move the barrel of potash to the factory basement, where there were three huge vats that were used to boil down sausage material. The corrosive chemicals were all dumped into the middle vat, and Luetgert turned on the steam beneath it, dissolving the material into liquid.

Combining this information with the eyewitness accounts, Captain Schuettler began to theorize about the crime. Circumstantial evidence seemed to show that Luetgert had killed his wife and boiled her in the sausage vats to dispose of the body. The more the policeman considered this, the more convinced he became that this was what had happened. Hoping to prove his theory, he and his men started another search of the sausage factory, and he soon made a discovery that became one of the most gruesome in the annals of Chicago crime.

On May 15, a search was conducted of the twelve-foot-long, five-foot-deep middle vat, which was two-thirds filled with a brownish, brackish liquid. The officers drained the greasy paste from the vat, using gunnysacks as filters, and began poking through the residue with sticks. Here Officer Walter Dean found several pieces of bone and two gold rings. One of them was a badly tarnished friendship ring, and the other was a heavy gold band engraved with the initials "L. L."

Louisa Luetgert had worn both of these rings.

When the bones were analyzed, they were found to be definitely human—a third rib; part of a humerus, the large bone in the upper arm; a bone from the palm of a hand; a bone from the fourth toe of a right foot; fragments of bone from a human ear; and a larger bone from a foot.

Adolph Luetgert, proclaiming his innocence, was arrested for the murder of his wife shortly after the search. Louisa's body was never found, and there were no witnesses to the crime, but police officers and prosecutors believed the evidence was overwhelming. Luetgert was indicted for the crime a month later, and details of the murder shocked the city's residents, especially those on the Northwest Side. Even though Luetgert was charged with boiling his wife's body, local rumor had it that she had been ground into sausage instead. Needless to say, sausage sales declined substantially in 1897.

Luetgert's first trial ended with a hung jury on October 21 after the jurors failed to agree on a suitable punishment. Some argued for the death penalty, while others voted for life in prison. Only one of the jurors thought that Luetgert might be innocent. A second trial was held, and on February 9, 1898, Luetgert was convicted and sentenced to a life term at Joliet Prison. He was taken away, still maintaining his innocence and claiming that he would receive another trial. He was placed in charge of meats in the prison's cold-storage warehouse, and officials described him as a model inmate.

By 1899, though, Luetgert began to speak less and less and often quarreled with the other convicts. He soon became a shadow of his former blustering persona, fighting for no reason and often babbling incoherently in his cell at night. His mind had been broken, either from guilt over his heinous crime or from the brutal conditions of the penitentiary.

Luetgert died in 1900, likely from heart trouble. The coroner who conducted the autopsy also reported that his liver was greatly enlarged and in such a condition of degeneration that "mental strain would have caused his death at any time."

The sausage factory stood empty for years, looming over the neighborhood as a grim reminder of the horrors that had visited there. The windows of the place became a target for rocks thrown from the nearby railroad embankment, and it often invited forays by the curious and the homeless.

In the months that followed his death, Luetgert's business affairs were entangled in litigation. The courts finally sorted everything out in August 1900, and a public auction was held for the factory and its grounds. Portions of the property were divided among several buyers, but the Library Bureau Company, which was founded by Dewey Decimal System creator Melvil Dewey, leased the factory itself. The company used it as a workshop and storehouse for its line of library furniture and office supplies. During the renovations, the infamous vats in the basement were discarded.

In June 1904, a devastating fire swept through the old sausage factory. It took more than three hours to put out the blaze, and when it was over, the building was still standing, but everything inside had been destroyed.

Despite the damage done to the building's interior, the Library Bureau reopened its facilities in the former sausage factory. It changed owners many times in the decades that followed. In 1907, a contracting mason purchased the old Luetgert house and moved it from behind the factory to another lot in the neighborhood, hoping to dispel the grim memories attached to it. The part of Hermitage Avenue that intersected with Diversey was closed. By the 1990s, the factory stood empty and crumbling, facing a collection of empty lots that were broken only by the occasional ramshackle frame house. In 1999, though, around the 100th anniversary of the death of Adolph Luetgert, the former sausage factory was converted into loft condominiums, and a brand new neighborhood sprang up to replace the aging homes that remained from the days of the Luetgerts. Fashionable brick homes and apartments appeared around the old factory, and run-down taverns were replaced with coffee shops.

The old neighborhood was gone, but the stories of this infamous crime still lingered, providing a unique place in history as the only Illinois murder that ever kept people from eating sausages.

CHAPTER 7
Chicago's Thrill Killers

On an afternoon in May 1924, the sons of two of Chicago's wealthiest and most illustrious families drove to the Harvard School on the city's South Side and kidnapped a young boy named Bobby Franks. Their plan was to carry out the "perfect murder." It was a scheme so devious that only two men of superior intellect—such as their own—could carry it out. These two men were Richard Loeb and Nathan Leopold. The privileged heirs of well-known Chicago families, they had embarked on a life of crime for fun and the pure thrill of it. They were also a pair of sexual deviants who considered themselves to be brilliant—a claim that would later lead to their downfall.

Nathan Leopold, or "Babe," as his friends knew him, was born in 1906 and from an early age had a number of sexual encounters, starting with the advances of a governess and culminating in a relationship with Richard Loeb. An excellent student with a genius IQ, he was only eighteen when he graduated from the University of Chicago. He was an expert ornithologist and botanist and spoke nine languages fluently. As was true of many future killers, his family life was totally empty and devoid of control. His mother had died when he was young, and his father gave him little personal attention, compensating for a lack of fatherly direction with expensive presents and huge sums of money. Leopold was given $3,000 to tour Europe before entering Harvard Law School, a car of his own, and a $125-a-week allowance.

Richard Loeb was the son of the vice president of Sears, Roebuck and Company. Although he was as wealthy as his friend was, Loeb was merely a clever young man and far from brilliant. He was, however, quite handsome and charming, and what he lacked in intelligence, he more than made up for in arrogance. Both young men were obsessed with perfection. To them, perfection meant being above all others, which their station in life endorsed. They felt they were immune to laws and criticism, which meant they were perfect.

Loeb fancied himself a master criminal detective, but his dream was to commit the perfect crime. With his more docile companion in tow, Loeb began developing what he believed to be the perfect scheme. He also constantly searched for ways to control others. Not long after the two became friends, Leopold attempted to initiate a sexual relationship with Loeb. At first Loeb spurned the other's advances, but then he offered a compromise: He would engage in sex with Leopold, but only under the condition that the other boy begin a career in crime with him. Leopold agreed, and they signed a formal pact to that effect.

Over the course of the next four years, they committed robbery, vandalism, arson, and petty theft, but this was not enough for Loeb.

He dreamed of something bigger. A murder, he convinced his friend, would be their greatest intellectual challenge.

They worked out a scheme over the next seven months. The plan was to kidnap someone and make it appear as though that person were being held for ransom. They would write the ransom note on a typewriter that had been stolen from Loeb's old fraternity house at the University of Michigan and make the family of the victim believe that he would be returned to them. Leopold and Loeb had no such plans, though—they intended to kill their captive.

In May 1924, they rented a car and drove to a hardware store at 43rd Street and Cottage Avenue, where they purchased some rope, a chisel, and a bottle of hydrochloric acid. They would garrote their victim, stab him with the chisel if necessary, and then destroy his identity with the acid.

The next day, they met at Leopold's home and wrapped the handle of the chisel with adhesive tape so that it offered a better grip. They gathered together a blanket and strips of cloth that could be used to wrap up and bind their victim. Leopold also placed a pair of wading boots in the car, because the boys planned to deposit the body in the swamps near Wolf Lake, located south of the city. They packed loaded pistols for both of them and looked over the already typed ransom note, which demanded $10,000 in cash. Neither of them needed the money, but they felt that the note would convince the authorities that the kidnappers were lowly criminals and deflect attention from people like themselves.

They had overlooked only one thing—a victim.

They first considered killing Loeb's younger brother, Tommy, but they discarded that idea, not because Tommy was a family member, but only because it would have been hard for Loeb to collect the ransom money without arousing suspicion. They thought about killing William Deutsch, grandson of millionaire and philanthropist Julius Rosenwald, but dismissed this idea as well because Rosenwald was the president of Sears and Loeb's father's immediate boss. They also came close to agreeing to kill their friend Richard Rubel, who regularly had lunch with them. He was ruled out, not because he was a good friend to them, but because they knew his father was cheap and would never agree to pay the ransom.

They could not agree on anyone but did feel that their victim should be small so that he could be easily subdued. With that in mind, they decided to check out the Harvard Preparatory School, which was located across the street from Leopold's home. They climbed into their rental car and began to drive. As they drove, Leopold noticed some boys near Ellis Avenue, and Loeb pointed out one of them that he recognized—fourteen-year-old Bobby Franks. Bobby was the son of millionaire Jacob Franks and a distant cousin of Loeb's. Chosen by chance, he would make the perfect victim for the perfect crime.

Bobby was already acquainted with his killers. He had played tennis with Loeb several times, and he happily climbed into the car. Although at their trial both denied being the actual killer, Leopold was at the wheel and Loeb was in the back, gripping the murder weapon tightly in his hands. They drove Bobby within a few blocks of the Franks residence in Hyde Park, and then Loeb suddenly grabbed the boy, stuffed a gag in his mouth, and smashed his skull four times with a chisel. The rope had been forgotten. Bobby collapsed onto the floor of the car, unconscious and bleeding badly.

When Leopold saw the blood spurting from Bobby's head, he cried out, "Oh God, I didn't know it would be like this!"

Loeb ignored him, intent on his horrific task. Even though Bobby was unconscious, Loeb stuffed his mouth with rags and wrapped him up in the heavy blanket. The boy continued to bleed for a time and then died.

With the excitement of the actual murder concluded, Leopold and Loeb casually drove south, stopped for lunch, and then drove for a little while longer. They had supper as they waited for the sun to go down. Eventually they ended up near a culvert along the Pennsylvania Railroad tracks that emptied into a swamp along Wolf Lake.

Leopold put on his hip boots and carried Bobby's body to the culvert. They had stripped all of the clothes from his body, and after dunking the boy's head underwater to make sure that he was dead, they poured acid on his face in hopes that he would be harder to identify. Leopold then struggled to shove the naked boy into the pipe and took his coat off to make the work easier. Unknown to the killers, a pair of eyeglasses were in the pocket of Leopold's coat, and they fell out into the water when he removed it. This would be the undoing of the "perfect crime."

After pushing the body as far into the pipe as he could, Leopold sloshed out of the mud toward the car, where Loeb waited for him. The killers believed that the body would not be found until long after the ransom money had been received. With darkness falling, though, Leopold failed to notice that Bobby's foot was dangling from the end of the culvert.

They drove back to the city and parked the rental car next to a large apartment building. Bobby's blood had soaked through the blanket he had been wrapped in and had stained the automobile's upholstery. The boys hid the blanket in a nearby yard and burned Bobby's clothing at Leopold's house. They typed the Frankses' address on the already prepared ransom note. After this, they hurried back to the car and drove to Indiana, where they buried the shoes that Bobby had worn and everything he had on him that was made from metal, including his belt buckle and class pin from the prep school.

Finally, their "perfect crime" carried out, they drove back to Leopold's home and spent the rest of the evening drinking and play-ing cards. Around midnight, they telephoned the Franks home and told Mr. Franks that he could soon expect a ransom demand for the return of his son. "Tell the police and he will be killed at once," they informed Mr. Franks. "You will receive a ransom note with instruc-tions tomorrow."

The next morning, the ransom note, signed "George Johnson," was delivered to the Frankses, demanding $10,000 in old, unmarked $10 and $20 bills. The money was to be placed in a cigar box that should be wrapped in white paper and sealed with wax. After the note's arrival, the Frankses' lawyer notified the police, who promised no publicity.

Meanwhile, Leopold and Loeb continued with the elaborate game they had concocted. They took the bloody blanket to an empty lot, burned it, and then drove to Jackson Park, where Loeb tore the keys out of his stolen typewriter. He threw the keys into one lagoon in the park and the typewriter into another. Later in the afternoon, Loeb took a train ride to Michigan City, leaving a note addressed to Bobby's parents in the telegram slot of a stationery desk in the train's observation car. He got off the train at 63rd Street, as it returned to the city, and rejoined the waiting Leopold. Andy Russo, a yardman, found the letter and sent it to the Frankses.

By the time the letter arrived, however, railroad maintenance men had already stumbled upon the body of Bobby Franks. The police notified Jacob Franks, who sent his brother-in-law to identify the body. He confirmed that it was Bobby, and the newspapers went into overdrive, producing "extra" editions that were on the street in a matter of hours.

One of the largest manhunts in the history of Chicago began. Witnesses and suspects were picked up in huge numbers, and slowly the "perfect crime" began to unravel. Despite their mental prowess, Leopold and Loeb were quickly caught. Leopold had dropped his eyeglasses near the spot where they hid the body, and the police traced the prescription to Albert Coe and Company, which stated that only three pairs of glasses with such unusual frames had been sold. One pair belonged to an attorney who was away in Europe, the second was owned by a woman, and the third had been bought by Nathan Leopold.

The boys were brought in for questioning and began supplying alibis for the time when Bobby had gone missing. They had been with two girlfriends, they claimed, "May" and "Edna." The police asked them to produce the girls, but the killers could not. Leopold claimed that he apparently had lost the glasses at Wolf Lake during a recent bird-hunting trip. The detectives noted that it had rained a few days before, but the glasses were clean. Could Leopold explain this? He couldn't.

Then two cub reporters, Al Goldstein and Jim Mulroy, obtained letters that Richard Loeb had written with the stolen typewriter—which had already been found in Jackson Park. The type on the letters matched that on the ransom note, and it was a perfect match with the typewriter that Leopold had "borrowed" from his fraternity house the year before.

Loeb broke first. He said that the murder was a lark, an experiment in crime to see whether the "perfect murder" could be carried out. He then denied being the killer and claimed that he had driven the car while Leopold had slashed Bobby Franks to death. Leopold refuted this. Finally the boys were brought together and admitted the truth: Loeb had been the killer and Leopold had driven the car, but both of them had planned the crime together—they were both guilty of the murder of Bobby Franks.

The people of Chicago and the rest of the nation were stunned. It was fully expected that the two would receive a death sentence for the callous and cold-blooded crime.

After the confession, Loeb's family disowned him, but Leopold's father turned to Clarence Darrow, America's most famous defense attorney, in hopes that he might save his son. For $100,000, Darrow agreed to seek the best possible verdict he could, which in this case was life in prison. "While the State is trying Loeb and Leopold," Darrow said, "I will try capital punishment."

Darrow would have less trouble with the case than he would with his clients, who constantly clowned around and hammed it up in the courtroom. The newspaper photographers frequently snapped photos of them smirking and laughing in court, and the public, already turned against them, became even more hostile toward the "poor little rich boys."

The lawyer was fighting an uphill battle, but he brought out every trick in the book and used shameless tactics during the trial.

He declared the boys to be insane. Leopold, he said, was a dangerous schizophrenic. They weren't criminals, he railed, they just couldn't help themselves. After this weighty proclamation, Darrow actually began to weep. The trial became a landmark in criminal law. He offered a detailed description of what would happen to the boys as they were hanged, providing a graphic image of bodily functions and physical pain. Darrow even turned to the prosecutor and invited him to perform the execution personally.

Darrow's horrifying description had a marked effect on the courtroom, and especially on the defendants. Loeb was observed to shudder, and Leopold got so hysterical that he had to be taken out of the courtroom. Darrow then wept for the defendants, wept for Bobby Franks, and finally wept for defendants and victims everywhere. He managed to get the best verdict possible out of the case. The defendants were given life in prison for Bobby Franks's murder and an additional ninety-nine years for his kidnapping.

Ironically, after all that, Darrow managed to get only $40,000 of his fee from Leopold's father, and this he got after a seven-month wait and the threat of a lawsuit.

Leopold and Loeb were sent to the Joliet Penitentiary. Even though the warden claimed they were treated just like all the other prisoners, they each enjoyed a private cell, books, a desk, a filing cabinet, and even pet birds. They also showered away from the other prisoners and took their meals, which were prepared to order, in the officers' lounge. Leopold was allowed to keep a flower garden. They were also permitted any number of unsupervised visitors. The doors to their cells were usually left open, and they had passes to visit one another at any time.

Richard Loeb was eventually killed by another inmate, toward whom he reportedly had been making sexual advances. The inmate, James Day, turned on him in a bathroom and attacked him with a razor. Loeb, covered in blood, managed to make it out of the bathroom and collapsed in the hallway. Guards found him bleeding in the corridor, and he died a short time later. It was later discovered that Day had slashed him fifty-six times with the razor.

Loeb's mother rushed to the prison with the family doctor when she heard what had happened, and Leopold waited anxiously by his friend's bedside. Loeb opened his eyes only one time. "I think I'm going to make it," he murmured, and then moments later, he died.

When Clarence Darrow was told of Loeb's death, he slowly shook his head. "He is better off dead," the great attorney said. "For him, death is an easier sentence."

Leopold lived on in prison for many years. It was said that he made many adjustments to his character, and some even believed he was completely rehabilitated. Even so, appeals for his parole were turned down three times. Finally, in 1958, poet Carl Sandburg, who even went so far as to offer Leopold a room in his home, pleaded his fourth appeal. In March of that year, he was released.

Leopold was allowed to go to Puerto Rico, where he worked among the poor and married a widow named Trudi Feldman Garcia de Quevedo, who owned a flower shop. He went on to write a book about his experiences called *Life Plus 99 Years* and continued to be hounded by the press for his role in the "perfect murder" he had committed decades before. He stated that he would be haunted by what he had done for the rest of his life.

Nathan Leopold died of heart failure on August 30, 1971, bringing an end to one of the most harrowing stories in the history of the city.

CHAPTER 8
The St. Valentine's Day Massacre

The rise of organized crime in Chicago began with the advent of Prohibition. The law that banned the sale and production of liquor went into effect in 1920, and criminal empires began to make vast fortunes. The decline of these empires began almost a decade later, in February 1929. It was on St. Valentine's Day of that year that the general public no longer saw the Mob as "public benefactors," offering alcohol to a thirsty city, but as the collection of killers and thugs that it truly was.

The St. Valentine's Day Massacre was not the death knell for the Mob in Chicago, nor was the subsequent destruction of the North Side Mob and the conviction of Al Capone for income tax evasion, but it was this bloody event that changed the face of crime in the city. In the years that followed, empires crumbled and lives were destroyed, bringing an end to the "glory days" of the Mob in Chicago.

The story of the Chicago Mob begins with one of the most important criminals in pre-Prohibition Chicago, Big Jim Colosimo. In addition to running a popular restaurant in the South Side Levee District, Colosimo was an influential brothel-keeper, and he maintained close ties to a number of important city officials. In this way, he ensured his political clout and his ability to operate his criminal enterprises without interference. By 1915, he was the acknowledged overlord of prostitution on the South Side.

While operating his string of whorehouses, Colosimo brought a young man named Johnny Torrio from New York to be his bodyguard and right-hand man. It was Torrio's ambitions that would lead to Colosimo's violent death. In 1920, Torrio wanted to expand the business into bootlegging, but Colosimo had no interest in this. His lack of forward thinking would lead to his downfall.

On the afternoon of May 11, 1920, Colosimo arrived at his restaurant, spoke with his secretary, and went into his office. Then, about 4:30 P.M., he allegedly took a telephone call from Johnny Torrio explaining that a shipment of whiskey was being delivered to the restaurant and that Colosimo had to sign for it personally. Colosimo left the office and walked out in the lobby. A moment later, two shots were fired. Colosimo's dead body was found lying on the floor of the lobby with a bullet wound to the back of the head. The second bullet was lodged in the plaster wall. From the angle of the shots, the police concluded that the killer must have been hiding in the cloakroom.

The funeral of Big Jim Colosimo was held on May 15 and was the first of the gaudy burial displays that were the fashion in Chicago's underworld throughout the 1920s. Thousands attended, including both gangsters and politicians, further underscoring the alliances between the two.

The murder of Colosimo remained a mystery, at least as far as legal evidence was concerned. Most everyone believed, though, that Johnny Torrio had carried out the murder in an effort to take over Colosimo's operation. Torrio quickly went to work, using a friend from New York as his muscle. That young man's name was Alphonse Capone.

Capone was born in Brooklyn in 1899 and made a name for himself as a slugger and a gunman with the famous Five Points Gang in New York, of which several of his cousins were members. Capone was only twenty-three when he came to Chicago, but Torrio soon promoted him to the post of manager in one of his toughest dives, the Four Deuces on South Wabash Avenue. During his time at the Four Deuces, Capone became Torrio's first lieutenant and chief gunman. In those days, he was rough and brutal, and there was little to indicate that he was destined for criminal greatness in the years to come. In the underworld, he was generally known as "Scarface Al Brown," a nickname based on the two parallel scars on his left cheek that he had received during a knife fight. Soon, however, his real name would be familiar to all of Chicago.

Torrio and Capone moved up quickly after Colosimo's death. The gangs on the South Side soon fell in line with their plans. Torrio's beer began to flow to the local gangs at $45 a barrel (each cost about $5 to produce). It was distributed on the South Side by Ragen's Colts and Ralph Sheldon's gang and on the West Side by the Circus Gang, led by Claude Maddox, as well as Marty Guilfoyle's gang and the Druggan-Lake Mob.

Up until 1922, the Chicago gangland remained at peace. But then the South Side O'Donnells, led by Spike O'Donnell, decided to rise up against Torrio. They were massacred back into their place over a period of about two years, between 1923 and 1925. Not long after, the Genna Brothers, who supplied Torrio with poorly made liquor that was manufactured in neighborhood stills, began to get greedy and demanded a larger piece of the action. Gang wars started to erupt. Most of the trouble seemed to come from the North Side Mob, an eccentric legion of mostly Irish gunmen led by Dion O'Banion. The high-quality Canadian liquor that was sent to Torrio by the Purple Gang in Detroit was constantly being hijacked by the North Siders. O'Banion also moved his bootlegging operation into

Cicero, which Torrio and Capone had already staked out as their exclusive territory.

Born Dean Charles O'Banion in 1892 in central Illinois, O'Banion spent the early years of his life in the small town of Maroa. Soon after the birth of his sister Ruth, his mother contracted tuberculosis and died in 1901. Dean was only nine years old at the time, and the loss was devastating to both him and his remaining family. They packed up and moved to Chicago. Dean, soon to be known as Dion, saw the end of his innocent years.

Upon moving to Chicago, O'Banion found himself turning to the streets for a playground. He became involved with a street gang known as the Little Hellions and began picking pockets and rolling drunks. At the same time, he sang in the choir and served as an altar boy at the Holy Name Cathedral. Some of the priests at the church believed that perhaps his devotion might lead to the priesthood, but O'Banion soon learned to ration his religion to Sundays and devote his remaining time to robbery and, as he reached young adulthood, burglary, what he called a "man's profession."

For a time, O'Banion worked as a singing waiter at the McGovern brothers' café and saloon on North Clark Street, crooning and balancing a hefty tray of beer glasses. McGovern's was a rough place and filled with crooks. It was here that O'Banion met, and befriended, notorious safecrackers and thieves such as George "Bugs" Moran, Earl "Hymie" Weiss, Vincent "The Schemer" Drucci, and Samuel "Nails" Morton. With these men at his side, O'Banion put together one of the most devastating gangs in Chicago. They centered their activities on the North Side, around the Lincoln Park neighborhood and the Gold Coast.

When Prohibition came along, O'Banion purchased several of the best breweries and distilleries on the North Side. While Capone and Torrio on the South Side were forced to import beer and whiskey at high prices or rely on rotgut produced by the Gennas to supply their outlets, O'Banion had the finest beer and booze available.

All over the city, society people and the owners of better restaurants bought from O'Banion. The quality of his product was better, and it was thought that he was more trustworthy than Capone, who was also running brothels and floating gambling operations. O'Banion publicly agreed to keep his operations north of the "dividing line" of Madison Street, but he still serviced his special customers on the South Side as well.

At first this encroachment on Capone-Torrio territory was tolerated. Capone attempted to negotiate with him, stating that if O'Banion ran booze on the South Side, then Capone should be allowed to have liquor warehouses in Lincoln Park. O'Banion refused—not because he couldn't deal with Capone, but because he was morally offended by Capone's involvement with prostitution. During the tenure of the O'Banion operation, and later the Weiss and Moran gangs, not one professional brothel operated in the opulent Northeast Side of Chicago. O'Banion's religious compunctions did not apply, however, to robberies, gambling casinos, hijacking Capone's trucks, or killing anyone who got in his way.

Torrio constantly tried to negotiate with O'Banion, rather than use the violence that Capone urged. Torrio and Capone held dozens of meetings with the North Siders, and each ended with the same results: O'Banion always promised to recognize Torrio's territory, but he never kept his word. Torrio knew, however, that if he killed O'Banion, it would mean all-out war in Chicago.

But his hesitation backfired on him in May 1924, when O'Banion told him that he planned to retire and wanted to sell Torrio his largest gambling den and his favorite brewery, Sieben's. Torrio agreed to buy up O'Banion's concerns and reportedly paid him half a million dollars in cash two days later. The gang leaders agreed to meet at Sieben's on May 19, as Torrio wanted to inspect his new property. He had not been there for more than ten minutes before Police Chief Morgan Collins, leading twenty officers, raided the place and arrested O'Banion, Hymie Weiss, and Torrio. This was Torrio's second arrest for violating Prohibition. He had been arrested once and fined in June 1923, but a second arrest could mean jail time—a fact of which O'Banion had been very much aware. Torrio also realized that O'Banion had no intention of retiring. He had conned Torrio into buying a brewery that he knew the police were about to shut down.

It was time, Torrio finally decided, to get rid of O'Banion. When Mike Merlo, founder and president of the powerful Unione Sicilian, died in November 1924, Torrio saw a way to kill the North Side gang leader. O'Banion was the owner of Schofield's Flower Shop, which was across the street from Holy Name Cathedral and was known as the only place to buy flowers for gangland funerals. Torrio would have his enemy killed in his own place.

On November 10, James Genna and Carmen Vacco entered O'Banion's flower shop and ordered a wreath for Merlo's funeral. They gave O'Banion $750 to pay for the arrangement. They told him that they would send some boys back to pick it up a little later and left the shop. Five minutes later, the telephone rang, and an unknown caller wanted to know if O'Banion had the flowers ready. He promised they would be ready at noon. At five minutes past the hour, a blue Jewett touring car pulled up in front of the shop.

One of the shop's employees, a black man named William Crutchfield, was sweeping up flower petals in the back room and looked up to see three men get out of the car and walk into the shop. Another man remained at the wheel of the vehicle.

O'Banion, dressed in a long white smock and holding a pair of florist's shears in his left hand, came out from behind the counter and extended his right hand in greeting. "Hello, boys," O'Banion said. "You from Mike Merlo's?"

Walking abreast, the three men approached O'Banion with smiles on their faces. The man in the center was tall and clean-shaven, and he wore an expensive overcoat and fedora. It was determined years later that this man was Frankie Yale. The other two, believed to be John Scalise and Albert Anselmi, were shorter and stockier, with dark complexions.

"Yes, for Merlo's flowers," Crutchfield heard Yale say before he stepped closer to O'Banion. Yale grabbed the other man's hand in greeting and pulled O'Banion toward him. The two men at his sides moved around him and drew pistols. Then, at close range, Yale rammed his own pistol into O'Banion's stomach and, holding his arm in a viselike grip, opened fire. All three men fired their weapons, and the bullets ripped into O'Banion. Two slugs struck him in the right breast, two hit him in the throat, and one passed through each side of his face. The shots were fired so close that powder burns were found at the opening of each wound. From that point on, this method of murder became known as the "Chicago handshake."

O'Banion fell, dead on his feet, into a display of geraniums. The three pistols that he had hidden on his body were unfired, not even drawn. The three men fled from the store and climbed into the car outside, which drove slowly away from the scene.

The murder was never solved. No arrests were ever made, and no one was ever indicted.

At an elaborate funeral service, O'Banion's friends filed past his body, tough gangsters weeping as they walked into Sbarbaro's Funeral Home. He was placed in a $10,000 bronze casket that had been fitted with bronze and silver double walls. A heavy plate-glass window had been fitted over O'Banion's patched-up face, and his men could peer down and see his head where it reclined on a white satin pillow.

O'Banion's funeral was the most lavish in Chicago gangland history. The hearse was led to Mount Carmel Cemetery by twenty-six trucks filled with flowers, worth more than $50,000. The scene at the cemetery was even more bizarre. On one side of the grave, lowering the body to rest, were Hymie Weiss, Bugs Moran, and Vincent Drucci; on the other were Al Capone, Johnny Torrio, and Angelo Genna. There was no violence at the funeral—that was still to come.

As Torrio suspected, O'Banion's death ignited an all-out war in Chicago. A few days after O'Banion's funeral, in November 1924, Torrio and his wife got out of a chauffeur-driven limousine in front of their house at 7011 Clyde Avenue, and Anna Torrio began to walk inside. As Torrio reached in to pick up some packages from their shopping trip, a black Cadillac screeched to a stop across the street. Inside, four men with pistols and shotguns watched for a moment, and then two of them, Moran and Weiss, jumped from the car and ran toward Torrio with their guns blazing.

Torrio fell immediately with a bullet in his chest and one in his neck. The other two men in the Cadillac, Drucci and Frank Gusenberg, jumped out and opened fire on the limousine with their shotguns. Meanwhile, Moran and Weiss ran to the fallen Torrio and, standing above him, fired bullets into his right arm and another into his groin. Moran leaned over to put the next one into Torrio's head, but his gun was empty. As he reached for another clip, Drucci began honking the horn of the Cadillac, signaling frantically that they needed to leave. Moran and Weiss ran to the car, and they sped away.

Somehow Torrio managed to crawl to the house, and his wife, who was screaming, came out and pulled him inside. A neighbor who had witnessed the shooting called an ambulance, and Torrio was raced to the hospital. Unbelievably, he survived, with a permanent scar on his neck. Reporters soon surrounded his hospital bed, demanding more information. Torrio stated that he knew all four of the assailants involved, but "I'll never tell their names," he said.

In February, Torrio, still bandaged, was sent to federal court for the Sieben's brewery fiasco and received a nine-month sentence to be served in the Waukegan County Jail, which had medical services for the ailing mobster. The treatment that Torrio received in prison was equal to that accorded someone with the status of a gangland boss. The windows of his cell were covered with bulletproof glass, and extra deputies guarded him day and night. Easy chairs, throw rugs, books, and other luxuries were added as well. Torrio also received the special privilege of taking his evening meals in the sheriff's home and being allowed to relax there on the front porch for a while each night, visiting with his wife and associates such as Al Capone.

As he served his time, Torrio had a lot of opportunity to think. When he got out, he announced that he was tired of the rackets and was turning his entire operation over to Capone. All he needed, he told his younger friend, was to get out of Chicago alive. Torrio and Anna left the city in an armor-plated limousine and were escorted by two roadsters filled with gunmen. When they reached a train station, just over the Indiana state line, Capone's men patrolled the station with machine guns until the train departed. The Torrios went to Florida and then on to Italy, living in Naples for three years.

Torrio got bored in Italy, but knowing he couldn't return to Chicago, he went to New York instead, where he went into the real estate business with the blessing of Meyer Lansky and Charles "Lucky" Luciano. He also helped establish a liquor cartel along the Atlantic Seaboard and established himself as an elder statesman of the underworld. He lived a sedate and quiet life after Prohibition was repealed, but in 1936, he was arrested for income tax evasion. After a series of trials and appeals, he served two years in Leavenworth and was paroled in 1941. He died of natural causes in a barber's chair in 1957.

Torrio's departure from Chicago shoved Al Capone into the violent spotlight of the Chicago underworld, and it also made him the top man in the city at only twenty-five years of age. He now had an annual income that eventually landed him a place in *The Guinness Book of World Records*. And he also had a bloody gang war on his hands.

Capone was sitting with his most trusted bodyguard, Frank Rio, in the restaurant of the Hawthorne Hotel in Cicero on September 20, 1926. The street outside was filled with shoppers and automobiles, and no one noticed at first as nine cars carrying North Side gangsters slowly cruised down 22nd Street. One of the cars accelerated away from the others, and as it passed the windows of the restaurant, black barrels of machine guns appeared from the windows and opened fire. Glass shattered and wood splintered as bullets riddled the restaurant. The car sped off and Rio jumped to his feet, gun in hand. But as Capone started to get up from the floor, his bodyguard pushed him back down, for he spotted the other cars in the procession.

The other eight touring cars were also full of men with machine guns. They opened fire on Capone's Cicero stronghold, emptying clip after clip into the hotel, spraying everything in sight. Hymie Weiss boldly climbed from his car, with Moran close behind him. Weiss ran up to the door of the hotel and opened fire with his machine gun, waving the weapon back and forth across the width of the passageway beyond the doors. When he finished firing, he walked coolly back to the car, and with honking and shouts, the North Siders drove away. More than 1,000 rounds had been fired into the building, and every window in the place was shattered. Amazingly, no one had been killed.

On October 11, Weiss was attending the murder trial of "Polack Joe" Saltis and his driver Frank "Lefty" Koncil, when he decided to take a break and return to his office above O'Banion's old flower shop. As Weiss drove toward the office along with gunman Patrick Murray, they had no idea that four machine gunners were waiting for them, hiding on the third floor of a nearby building. Weiss was a marked man as soon as he left his car on Superior Street, just south of the Holy Name Cathedral. He approached the flower shop with Murray by his side. At the deafening sound of machine guns, the pedestrians on the street scattered.

Murray died instantly. Weiss took ten bullets and survived long enough to be pronounced dead without regaining consciousness at Henrotin Hospital. Meanwhile, the assassins fled their third-floor lair, exited the rear of the building, and disappeared into the crowds along Dearborn Street. A discarded machine gun was found in an alley off Dearborn, but it couldn't be traced back to the killers.

Police Chief Collins issued a gruff statement: "I don't want to encourage the business, but if somebody has to be killed, it's a good thing the gangsters are murdering themselves off. It saves trouble for the police."

The other partners in the North Side Gang were wiped out, or fled Chicago, one by one, eventually leaving only Bugs Moran.

George Moran was born in Minnesota in 1893 but moved to Chicago with his parents around the turn of the century. Here he joined up with one of the North Side Irish gangs and was befriended by Dion O'Banion. The two began working together, robbing warehouses, but after one fouled-up job, Moran was captured. He kept his silence and served two years in Joliet prison without implicating O'Banion in the crime. He was released at age 19 and went back to work with his friend. He was soon captured again and once more kept silent about who he worked with. He stayed in jail this time until 1923.

When Moran, known as "Bugs" because of his quick temper, got out of prison, he joined up with O'Banion's now formidable North Side Mob. They had become a powerful organization, supplying liquor to Chicago's wealthy Gold Coast. Moran became a valuable asset, hijacking Capone's liquor trucks at will. He became known as O'Banion's right-hand man, always impeccably dressed, right down to the two guns that he always wore. When O'Banion was killed in his flower shop in 1924, Moran swore revenge. The war that followed claimed many lives and by 1927, Moran stood alone against the Capone Mob, most of his allies having succumbed in the fighting.

He continued to taunt his powerful enemy, always looking for ways to destroy him. In early 1929, Moran sided with Joe Aiello in another war against Capone. He and Aiello reportedly gunned down Pasquillano Lolordo, one of Capone's men, and Capone vowed that he would have Moran wiped out on February 14. He was living on his estate outside of Miami at the time and put in a call to Chicago. Capone had a very special "valentine" that we wanted delivered to Moran.

Through a contact, Capone arranged for someone to call Moran and tell him that a special shipment of hijacked whiskey was going to be delivered to one of Moran's garages on the North Side. Moran's friend, Adam Heyer, owned the garage and it was used as a distribution point for North Side liquor. A sign out front read "S-M-C Cartage Co. Shipping - Packing - Long Distance Hauling." It was located at 2122 North Clark Street.

On the morning of February 14, a group of Moran's men gathered at the Clark Street garage. One of the men was Johnny May, an ex-safecracker who had been hired by Moran as an auto mechanic. He was working on a truck that morning, with his dog, a German shepherd named Highball, tied to the bumper. In addition, six other men waited for the truck of hijacked whiskey to arrive. The men were Frank and Pete Gusenberg; James Clark, Moran's brother-in-law; Adam Heyer; Al Weinshank; and Reinhardt Schwimmer, a young optometrist who had befriended Moran and hung around the liquor warehouse just for the thrill of rubbing shoulders with gangsters.

Moran was already late for the morning meeting. He was due to arrive at 10:30 but didn't even leave for the rendezvous, in the company of Willie Marks and Ted Newberry, until several minutes after that.

While the seven men waited inside of the warehouse, they had no idea that a police car had pulled up outside, or that Moran had spotted the car as he was driving south on Clark Street. Rather than deal with what he believed was a shakedown, Moran stopped at the next corner for a cup of coffee.

Five men got out of the police car, two of them in uniforms and three in civilian clothing. They entered the building, and a few moments later the clatter of machine gun fire broke the stillness of the snowy morning. Soon after, five figures emerged and they drove away. May's dog, inside of the warehouse, began barking and howling.

The landlady in the next building, Mrs. Jeanette Landesman, was bothered by the sound of the dog and she sent one of her boarders, C. L. McAllister, to the garage to see what was going on. He came outside two minutes later, his face a pale white color. He ran frantically up the stairs to beg Mrs. Landesman to call the police. He cried that the garage was full of dead men!

The police were quickly summoned; on entering the garage, they were stunned by the carnage. Moran's men had been lined up against the rear wall of the garage and had been sprayed with machine guns. Pete Gusenberg had died kneeling, slumped over a chair. James Clark had fallen on his face with half of his head blown away, and Heyer, Schwimmer, Weinshank, and May were thrown lifeless onto their backs. Only one of the men survived the slaughter and only for a few hours. Frank Gusenberg had crawled from the blood-sprayed wall where he had fallen and ended up out in the middle of the dirty floor. He was rushed to the Alexian Brothers Hospital, barely hanging on. Police sergeant Clarence Sweeney leaned down close to him and asked who had shot him.

"No one—nobody shot me," he groaned. Gusenberg died later that night.

Police canvassed Clark Street between Webster and Garfield (now Dickens) Avenues. In 1929, this was largely a district of rooming houses, and there were dozens of landlords and tenants to interview. Transients came and went, the detectives were told, but a couple of women did remember that teams of suspicious men had recently rented rooms with street views for $8 per day.

The death toll of the massacre stood at seven but the killers had missed Moran. When the police contacted him later and asked who had sent the men to the garage, he "raved like a madman." To the newspapers, Moran targeted Capone as ordering the hit. He proclaimed: "Only Capone kills guys like that."

The murders broke the power of the North Side Gang. Though there have been many claims as to who the actual shooters were that day, most likely they included Scalise, Anselmi, and "Machine Gun" Jack McGurn, all of whom were some of Capone's most trusted men. All three men were arrested, along with Joseph Guinta, but McGurn had an alibi, and Scalise and Guinta were killed before they could be tried.

The St. Valentine's Day Massacre marked the end of any significant gang opposition to Capone, but it was also the act that finally began the decline of Capone's criminal empire. He had just gone too far, and the authorities, and even Capone's adoring public, were ready to put an end to the bootleg wars. The massacre started a wave of reform that would get Capone out of power for good.

In May 1929, Capone was summoned to New York to meet with Meyer Lansky and Charles "Lucky" Luciano, who were in the process of forming a national crime syndicate. They were unhappy with the attention Capone had attracted in Chicago and had decided that it would be good public relations if Al Capone went to jail for a time. It was arranged for him to be arrested in Philadelphia on a charge of carrying a concealed weapon. Two detectives were paid $10,000 each to arrest him in the lobby of a movie theater, charge him, and get him sentenced as quickly as possible. It all happened in just sixteen hours, and he was sentenced to spend a term of one year at Eastern State Penitentiary.

Capone continued to conduct business from prison. He was given a private cell and allowed to make long-distance telephone calls from the warden's office and to meet with his lawyers and with Frank Nitti, Jake Guzik, and his brother Ralph Capone, all of whom made frequent trips to Philadelphia. He was released two months early on good behavior, but when he returned to Chicago in March 1930, he found himself branded "public enemy number one."

The climate of the city had changed considerably during the time Capone had been away. His popularity had waned, and the police were adamant about putting his operation out of business. Police Captain John Stege even posted a guard of twenty-five policemen in front of the Capone home on Prairie Avenue, with orders to arrest him as soon as he arrived from Pennsylvania. Capone slipped quietly into the city, though, and took up residence at the Hawthorne Inn in Cicero, where he spent four days answering mail and getting caught up on the state of operations. Then he and his attorneys blatantly called on Captain Stege and the U.S. district attorney and found that neither of them had an actual warrant for his arrest. With that settled, he returned to Chicago.

Although no charges had actually been filed against Capone, there was nothing to prevent the police from keeping him under surveillance. Two uniformed policemen were assigned to follow Capone everywhere he went, day and night. Capone's empire was starting to crumble.

The U.S. government had now gotten involved in Chicago's problem of how to get rid of Al Capone. Washington dispatched a group of Treasury agents—Eliot Ness and his "Untouchables"—to harass Capone and try to find a way to bring down his operation. In the end, it was not murder or illegal liquor that got Capone; it was income tax evasion. He was arrested on October 6, 1931, and indicted. On October 17, he was convicted on five counts: three of evading taxes from 1925 to 1928 and two of failing to file tax returns in 1928 and 1929. Sentenced to spend eleven years in a federal prison, he was first sent to Atlanta, and then in 1934 was transferred to the brutal, "escapeproof" prison known as Alcatraz.

This prison was a place of total punishment and few privileges. Many of the prisoners at Alcatraz went insane from the harsh conditions, and Capone was probably one of them. The beatings, attempts on his life, and prison routine took a terrible toll on Capone's mind. After he was nearly stabbed to death in the yard, he was excused from outdoor exercise and usually stayed inside and played a banjo that was given to him by his wife. He later joined the four-man prison band. After five years, though, Capone's mind snapped. He often refused to leave his cell and sometimes crouched down in the corner and talked to himself. Another inmate recalled that on some days, Capone simply made and remade his bunk all day long. He spent the last portion of his stay in the prison hospital ward, being treated for an advanced case of syphilis. He left Alcatraz in 1939 and died in Florida in 1947.

The February 1929 massacre may have been the beginning of the end for Al Capone, and it began the decline of Bugs Moran as well. With the remnants of his gang, Moran attempted to take back control of the Gold Coast, but Capone's men were too powerful.

Moran's lot did improve somewhat after Capone went to prison in 1931, but this didn't last long.

The end of World War II reduced the once powerful gangster to petty burglaries. He moved to downstate Illinois, St. Louis, and then Ohio before a failed robbery got him arrested by the FBI. Moran was sentenced to serve ten years in prison in 1946 and upon his release was quickly rearrested for another robbery. This time he was sent to Leavenworth, where he died from lung cancer in February 1957. It was a sad, and almost pathetic, ending for the gangster who was known after St. Valentine's Day 1929 as "the man who got away."

CHAPTER 9
Farewell to the Grimes Sisters

Along a quiet roadway on the far Southwest Side of Chicago, the innocence of the region came to an end with the heartbreaking discovery of the bodies of two girls. What had happened to them became one of the Chicagoland's most puzzling unsolved mysteries.

On December 28, 1956, Patricia Grimes, age thirteen, and her sister Barbara, fifteen, left their home at 3624 South Damon Avenue and headed for the Brighton Theater, only a mile away. Both avid fans of Elvis Presley, the sisters were going to see his film *Love Me Tender* for the eleventh and final time. The girls were recognized in the popcorn line at 9:30 P.M. and then seen on an eastbound Archer Avenue bus at 11 P.M. After that, things became less certain, and this may have been the last time they were ever seen alive. The two sisters were missing for twenty-five days before their naked and frozen bodies were found along German Church Road, just outside the small town of Willow Springs.

The girls' mother, Loretta Grimes, expected them to be home by 11:45 P.M. but was already growing uneasy when they had not arrived fifteen minutes prior to that. At midnight, she sent another daughter, Theresa, and her son Joey to the bus stop at 35th and Hoyne to watch for them. After three buses had stopped and failed to discharge their sisters, Theresa and Joey returned home without them. They never saw the girls again, but strangely, others claimed they had.

Further reported sightings of the two girls came from classmates who said they spotted them at Angelo's Restaurant at 3551 South Archer Avenue more than twenty-four hours after their disappearance. It is not known how accurate this sighting was, as a railroad conductor also claimed he saw them on a train near the Great Lakes Naval Training Center in north suburban Glenview around the same time. A security guard on the Northwest Side offered directions to two girls he believed were the Grimes sisters on the morning of December 29, hours after they disappeared. On January 1, both girls were allegedly identified as passengers aboard a Chicago Transit Authority bus on Damen Avenue. During the week that followed, they were reported in Englewood by George Pope, a night clerk at the Unity Hotel on West 61st Street, who refused them a room because of their ages. Three employees at Kresge believed they saw the girls listening to Elvis Presley songs at the record counter on January 3.

Though the police theorized that the girls had run away, Loretta Grimes refused to believe it. She was sure the girls had gone missing against their will, but the authorities were not convinced. Regardless, it became the greatest missing-persons hunt in Chicago police history. Even Elvis Presley, in a statement issued from Graceland, asked the girls to come home and ease their mother's worries. The plea went unanswered.

More strange things occurred before the bodies of the girls were found. A series of ransom letters, which were later discovered to have come from a mental patient, took Mrs. Grimes to Milwaukee on January 12. She was escorted by FBI agents and instructed to sit in a downtown Catholic church with $1,000 on the bench beside her. The letter promised that Barbara Grimes would walk in to retrieve the money and leave to deliver it to the kidnapper. She and her sister would then be released. But no one ever came, and Mrs. Grimes was left sitting for hours to contemplate her daughters' fate. By that time, it's likely that the bodies of the two girls were already lying along German Church Road, covered with snow.

But if that's true, then how does one explain two telephone calls received by Wallace and Ann Tollstan on January 14? Their daughter Sandra was a classmate of Patricia's at the St. Maurice School, and the Tollstans received the two calls around midnight. The first call jolted Mr. Tollstan out of his sleep, but when he picked up the receiver, the person on the other end of the line did not speak. He waited a few moments and then hung up. About fifteen minutes later, the phone rang again, and this time Ann Tollstan answered it. The voice on the other end of the line asked, "Is that you, Sandra? Is Sandra there?" But before Mrs. Tollstan could bring her daughter to the phone, the caller had clicked off the line. Ann Tollstan was convinced that the frightened voice on the telephone had belonged to Patricia Grimes.

And that wasn't the only strange happening to mark the period when the girls were missing. On January 15, a police switchboard operator received a call from a man who refused to identify himself but insisted that the girls' bodies would be found in a park at 81st and Wolf. He claimed that this revelation had come to him in a dream and then hung up. The call was traced to Green's Liquor Market on South Halsted, and the caller was discovered to be Walter Kranz, a fifty-year-old steamfitter. He was taken into custody after the bodies were found a week later—less than a mile from the park that Kranz said he had dreamed of. He became one of numerous people who were questioned by the police and then released.

The search for the Grimes sisters ended on January 22, 1957, when construction worker Leonard Prescott was driving south on German Church Road early one morning. He spotted what appeared to be two discarded clothing-store mannequins lying next to a guardrail, a short distance from the road. A few feet away, the ground dropped off to Devil's Creek below. Unsure of what he had seen, Prescott nervously brought his wife, Marie, to the spot, and then they drove to the local police station. Marie was so upset by the sight of the bodies that she had to be carried back to their car.

Once investigators realized the "mannequins" were actually bodies, they soon discovered they were the Grimes sisters. Barbara lay on her left side, with her legs slightly drawn up toward her body. Her head was covered by the body of her sister, who had been thrown onto her back with her head turned sharply to the right. It looked as if they had been discarded there by someone so cold and heartless that he saw the girls as nothing more than refuse to be tossed away on a lonely roadside.

The officials in charge, Cook County Sheriff Joseph D. Lohman and Harry Glos, an aggressive investigator for the coroner, Walter E. McCarron, surmised that the bodies had been lying there for several days, perhaps as far back as January 9. This had been the date of the last heavy snowfall, and the frigid temperatures that followed the storm had preserved the bodies in a state that resembled how they looked at the moment of death.

The bodies discovered along German Church Road sent the various police departments into action. A short time after they were found, more than 160 officers from Chicago, Cook County, the forest preserves, and five south suburban police departments began combing the woods—and tramping all over whatever evidence may have been there. Between the officers, the reporters, the medical examiners, and everyone else, the investigation was off to a bad start.

The investigation became even more confusing in the days to come. The bodies were removed from the scene and taken to the Cook County Morgue, where they would be stored until they thawed out and an autopsy became possible. Before they were removed, though, both police investigators and reporters commented on the condition of the corpses, noting bruises and marks that still have not been adequately explained to this day. According to a newspaper article, there were three ugly wounds in Patricia's abdomen, and the left side of her face had been battered, resulting in a possibly broken nose. Barbara's face and head had also been bruised, and her chest had punctures from an ice pick. Once the bodies were moved, investigators stayed on the scene to search for clothing and clues but found nothing.

The autopsies were performed the following day, and all hope that the examinations would provide new evidence or leads was quickly dashed. Despite the efforts of three experienced pathologists, they could not agree on a time or cause of death. They stated that the girls had died from shock and exposure but were able to reach this conclusion only by eliminating other causes. They also concluded that the girls had died on December 28, the night they had disappeared, creating more mysteries than they had managed to solve. If the girls had died on the night they had gone missing, then how could the reported sightings after that date be explained? And if the bodies had been exposed to the elements since that time, then why hadn't anyone else seen them?

Barbara and Patricia were buried on January 28, one month after they disappeared, although the mysteries surrounding what had happened to them were no closer to being solved than they had been in December.

The residents of Chicagoland were stunned, and the case of the murdered girls became an obsession. The local community organized a search for clues, and volunteers passed out flyers looking for information.

The *Chicago Tribune* invited readers to send in theories about the case and paid $50 for any they published. The clergy and parishioners from St. Maurice, where the Grimes family attended church, offered a $1,000 reward and sent letters to area residents, hoping that someone might have seen the girls before they vanished. Photographs were even taken of friends of the girls in clothing similar to what the sisters had worn on December 28, in hopes that it might jog the memory of someone who saw them. On the night they went to see *Love Me Tender* for the last time, Patricia had on blue jeans, a yellow sweater, a black jacket with white sleeve stripes, a white scarf over her head, and black shoes. Her sister reportedly wore a gray tweed skirt, yellow blouse, three-quarter-length coat, gray scarf, white bobby socks, and black ballerina shoes. The clothing, though, like the girls' killer, was never found.

The killer may have eluded the authorities, but it was not because no one was trying to find him or her. Investigators questioned an unbelievable 300,000 individuals, searching for information about the girls, and 2,000 of these people were rigorously interrogated, which in those days could be brutal. A number of suspects were seriously considered, and among the first was the "dreamer," Walter Kranz, who had called police with his mysterious tip on January 15. He was held at the Englewood police station for some time and was repeatedly interrogated and given lie detector tests about his involvement in the murders. No solid evidence was ever found against him, though.

The police also picked up a seventeen-year-old named Max Fleig as a suspect, but the law at that time did not allow juveniles to be tested with a polygraph. Police Captain Ralph Petaque persuaded the boy to take the test anyway, and in the midst of it, he confessed to kidnapping the girls. Because the test was illegal and inadmissible, the police were forced to let Fleig go free. Was he the killer? No one will ever know. Fleig was sent to prison a few years later for the brutal murder of another young woman, but whether he had any connection to the death of the Grimes sisters remains a mystery.

In the midst of all of this, the police still had to deal with nuts and cranks, more so-called psychic visions, and a number of false confessions, which made their work even harder.

Eager to crack the floundering case, Sheriff Lohman then arrested a skid-row dishwasher named Edward L. "Benny" Bedwell. The drifter, who sported Elvis-style sideburns and a ducktail haircut, had reportedly been seen with the Grimes sisters in a restaurant where he sometimes washed dishes in exchange for food. When he was initially questioned, Bedwell admitted that he had been in the D&L Restaurant on West Madison with two girls and an unnamed friend, but he insisted that the owners of the place were mistaken about the girls being the Grimes sisters.

According to the owners, John and Minnie Duros, the group had entered the diner around 5:30 A.M. on the morning of December 30. They described the taller girl, who Minnie said was wearing a coat with the name "Pat" embroidered on it, as being either so drunk or so sick that she was staggering as she walked. The couples sat in a booth for a while, listened to Elvis songs on the jukebox, and then went outside. One of the girls came back in, laid her head on the table, and seemed to be sick. The two men eventually managed to get her outside, and all of them left together. One of the girls told Minnie that they were sisters.

Lohman found the story plausible, thanks to the unshakable identification of the girls by Minnie Duros, their respective heights, the fact that one of them said they were sisters, and finally, Bedwell's resemblance to Elvis. Lohman believed this might have been enough to get the girls to go along with him. And then there was Bedwell's confession, which related a lurid and sexually explicit tale of drunken debauchery with the two young women. He made and recanted three confessions and even reenacted the crime for investigators on January 27.

Everyone doubted the story but Lohman. He booked Bedwell on murder charges, but the drifter's testimony was both vague and contradictory. On January 31, he testified that he had confessed out of fear of Lohman's men, who he said had struck and threatened him while he was being questioned. Lohman denied that Bedwell had been beaten and told newspapers that the drifter had lied when he contradicted his confession, adding that he considered him the prime suspect in the case.

The case against Bedwell further unraveled when his friend was identified as William C. Williamson, who ended up in jail on charges of drunkenness soon after his meeting with Bedwell and the two girls at the Duros's diner. He admitted that he was with Bedwell and two girls but denied that they were the Grimes sisters.

State's attorney Benjamin Adamowski ordered the drifter released. Bedwell later spent time in prison on a weapons charge and died at some point after he was released in 1986.

The dismissal of charges against Bedwell in the Grimes case set off another round of bickering among police departments and various jurisdictions, and the case became even more mired in red tape and inactivity. It got even worse when coroner's investigator Harry Glos publicly criticized the autopsy findings concerning the time and cause of death. He shocked the public by announcing that Barbara and Patricia could not have died on the night they disappeared, saying that an ice layer around the bodies proved that they were warm when they were left along German Church Road, and that only after January 7 would there have been enough snow to create the ice and hide the bodies.

Glos also raised the issues of the puncture wounds and bruises on the bodies, which had never been explained or explored. He was sure that the girls had been violently treated prior to death and also asserted that the older sister, Barbara, had been sexually molested before she was killed. The pathologists had denied this, but the Chicago police crime lab reluctantly confirmed it. They were angry with Glos, however, for releasing the information.

The coroner, Walter McCarron, promptly had Glos fired, and many of the other investigators in the case accused him of being reckless and of political grandstanding. Only Sheriff Lohman, who later deputized Glos to work on the case without pay, remained on his side. He agreed that the girls had likely been beaten and tortured by a sexual predator who lured them into the kidnap car under a seemingly innocent pretense. Lohman remained convinced until his death in 1969 that the predator who had killed the girls had been Benny Bedwell.

Other theories maintained that the girls indeed encountered Bedwell or another older man, and rumors circulated that the reputation of the two girls had been polished to cover up some very questionable behavior on their part. It was said that they sometimes hung around a bar on Archer Avenue where men would buy them drinks. One of the men may have been Benny Bedwell. Harry Glos, who died in 1994, released information that one of the girls had been sexually active, and later reports from those who have seen the autopsy slides say there is evidence that both of them may have been. It is believed that coroner McCarron may have decided not to release this because of religious reasons or to spare additional grief for the family.

Today veteran detectives believe that there was much more to the story than met the eye. The general consensus seems to be that Barbara and Patricia may have been abducted by a front man for a "white slavery" ring and taken to a remote location in the woods surrounding Willow Springs. They are convinced that the girls were strangled after refusing to become prostitutes. It's also possible that the girls may have been lured into an involvement in a prostitution ring by someone they knew, not realizing what would be required of them, and were killed to keep them silent.

Others refused to even consider this, though, and were angered by the negative gossip about the two girls. Some remain angry about this even today, maintaining that Barbara and Patricia were nice, ordinary, happy girls who were tragically killed on a cold night because they made the mistake of accepting a ride from a stranger. They didn't hang around in bars, these old friends maintain. They were simply innocent teenage girls, just like everyone else at that time.

Perhaps those old acquaintances were right. There are few stories as tragic as the demise of the Grimes sisters, and perhaps it provides some cold comfort for us to believe that their death was simply a terrible mistake or due to the actions of deviant killer. But does believing that the girls were simply in the wrong place at the wrong time, and that such a thing could have happened to anyone, make us feel better—or worse?

Now, fifty years later, the mystery of who killed the Grimes sisters remains unsolved. As there is no statute of limitations for murder, the case officially remains open, but hope of any closure has dimmed over the years, and the murderer's trail has gone tragically cold.

CHAPTER 10
Born to Raise Hell

On the hot summer night of July 13, 1966, a brutal and dim-witted drifter butchered his way into the annals of Chicago crime with the murders of eight nursing students on the Southeast Side. From that point on, the name of Richard Speck struck terror into the hearts of young women living alone, and few would ever forget the words inked onto his arm as a burning tattoo.

"Born to Raise Hell," the tattoo read, and it was a fitting description of his life.

Richard Speck was born in Kirkwood in December 1941, the seventh of eight children. Over the years, dozens have speculated about the reason behind Speck's brutal crimes and whether he turned evil somewhere along the way or was simply born bad—as the tattoo scrawled on his arm claimed. Many have also wondered if perhaps things might have turned out differently in the lives of eight nursing students if Speck's father, whom he adored, had not died when the boy was only six years old. Speck was raised by his mother in a strict Baptist setting that forbade alcohol and worldly influences. She later married Carl Lindberg, a violent man with an arrest record, and they moved to Dallas, Texas, where Lindberg began taking out his drunken rages on his stepson. By this time, Speck was a slow-witted failure with schoolwork and on the fast track to nowhere. He started running with some older boys, drinking, fighting, and getting into trouble.

In November 1962, Speck married Shirley Malone, and they had a daughter, Bobby Lynn, soon after. Their married bliss was short-lived, however, and Speck began abusing both his wife and his mother-in-law. According to Shirley's later accounts, he often raped her at knifepoint, claiming that he needed sex four to five times each day. Likely to Shirley's relief, Speck ended up in jail for theft and check fraud in 1963. He was paroled in January 1965, but after only four weeks, he was arrested again for aggravated assault. He was sentenced to serve another sixteen months but was released after just six. Shirley filed for divorce in January 1966.

When Speck was arrested again for burglary and assault, he fled from Dallas with the help of his sister Carolyn and left for Chicago. He showed up at the home of another sister, Martha, and his brother-in-law Gene Thornton. Speck announced his intention of searching for work as a merchant seaman, but after he did nothing for several days, Thornton got frustrated and drove his unwanted houseguest to the National Maritime Union Hall, located at 2315 East 100th Street. The building was just a few doors away from three residential townhouses, including number 2319, which had been rented by the South Chicago Community Hospital for 24 of its 155 student nurses.

Thornton brought Speck to the Maritime Union Hall in the hope that there was still an open berth on a ship that was bound for Vietnam. The position went to a man with greater seniority, leaving

Speck without a spot. Disappointed, but unwilling to take Speck back in, Thornton handed him $25 and wished him well. He then drove off and left his brother-in-law to fend for himself.

A short time later, Speck managed to get a position aboard an iron ore ship on the Great Lakes, where he was stricken with appendicitis and hospitalized in Hancock, Michigan. When he returned to Chicago in mid-June, he was fired for being drunk and disorderly. He had been warned repeatedly about his drinking and violent behavior, but he disregarded the threats. After that he spent the next three weeks in cheap hotels and sleeping in the park, financing his liquor and his visits to prostitutes with whatever odd jobs he could find.

On July 13, a depressed and angry Speck was drinking heavily in the Shipyard Inn on the Southeast Side. After a volatile combination of pills and liquor, he suddenly got the urge to "raise some hell." He later said that he remembered nothing after this point.

Leaving the bar with a hunting knife, a pocketknife, and a borrowed .22-caliber pistol, Speck walked over to one of the nearby student dormitories. For the past several weeks, the drifter had seen the women coming and going from the buildings, sunbathing in Luella Park, and walking back and forth to their classes. He was familiar enough with their schedules to know that at nearly 11 P.M., they would be home in bed.

Corazon Amurao, who shared a second-floor bedroom with two other young women, answered a loud knock on the townhouse door. She found a tall, lean stranger standing on the doorstep. He smelled of liquor and had a knife in one hand and a gun in the other. He slurred that he was not going to hurt her. "I'm only going to tie you up," he said. "I need money to go to New Orleans."

He shoved his way into the townhouse and ordered the three Filipino students, Valentina Paison, Merlita Garguilo, and Corazon, into a bedroom at the back of the building, where Pamela Wilkening, Nina Schmale, and Pat Matusek were getting ready for bed. Speck took the sheets from the beds and cut them into strips, which he used to bind the women by their wrists and ankles. At 11:30, a seventh nurse, Gloria Davy, returned home from a date and was also tied up. Then, half an hour later, Suzanne Farris and her friend Mary Ann Jordan came to the front door. Speck pulled them inside and led them into the back bedroom at gunpoint.

In the course of an hour, Speck had systematically tied and gagged each of the women. How he managed to do this with almost no resistance remains one of the great unsolved mysteries in Chicago crime. Why did none of the women try to escape? Why didn't they try to overpower Speck as he was tying another victim? Why didn't any of the women in the other townhouses hear anything that was taking place? No one knows, and to this day these things remain a mystery.

By 3:30 A.M., Speck's lust was finally spent. One by one, he had taken eight of the young women out of the bedroom and killed them. Only one of them, Gloria Davy, had been raped, but all were dead—save for Cora Amurao, who had managed to roll under a bunk bed and cowered there in fear and shock until Speck finally left. Amurao remained hidden, frozen in terror, until nearly 6 in the morning. When she finally emerged from her hiding place, she climbed out of the apartment window and, perched on a ledge, began to scream.

Her screams caught the attention of Judy Dykton, a student who lived across the street. She had gotten up early to study and was startled by the cries from outside. Snatching her robe, she ran over to find Cora shaking and crying on the window ledge. Judy entered the open door of the townhouse and stepped into the living room. She first discovered the naked body of Gloria Davy, her hands tied behind her and a strip of cloth wrapped tightly around her throat. Her skin had turned cold and a dusty blue color. She was obviously dead. Judy turned and fled to the apartment of the housemother, Mrs. Bisone.

The housemother woke up the other student nurses and ran from the house toward 2319. With her she brought Leona Bonczak, who entered the house. Leona first checked to see if Gloria showed any signs of life, and then mounted the stairs and looked down the hall. In the bathroom, she found the body of Pat Matusek and then crept into the other bedrooms, where she discovered the rest of the students so drenched in blood that she was unable to recognize any of them, save for Nina Schmale. A pillow covered most of the girl's face, and she lay on her back, hands tied behind her, a cloth around her neck, legs spread apart—and a fatal knife wound to her heart.

Stunned, Leona went downstairs and numbly told Mrs. Bisone that everyone was dead. The housemother, shaking and sick, picked up the phone, called South Chicago Community Hospital, and told them that all of her girls had been murdered. When the hospital asked her who had been killed, she was unable to tell them. The only words she uttered were "Send help!"

Someone on the street managed to flag down Officer Daniel Kelly, a young patrolman who had been on the job for only eighteen months. After radioing in that there was trouble, he entered the house. He was shocked to discover the body of Gloria Davy in the living room. Kelly had once dated Gloria's sister. Upset, he drew his gun, searched the place, and found the other bodies. The townhouse looked like a charnel house, and in places, the blood in the carpeting was so thick that it pooled over Kelly's shoes. He ran outside to his car radio and called in to report what he had found. Soon Kelly heard the comforting sounds of approaching sirens beginning to fill the air.

The street outside filled with police cars and cops, and people ran from door to door, alerting their neighbors of the horror found in 2319. The first detective on the scene was Jack Wallenda, who entered the house and viewed the bodies one by one. He was shocked by the utter brutality of the killings.

He found Gloria first. Belly down on the couch, she was nude and tied with double-knotted bedsheets. He noticed what appeared to be semen between her buttocks and found buttons from her blouse strewn down the stairs. The killer apparently had torn her clothes off as he pulled her to the living room. Also tossed on the floor was a man's white T-shirt, size 38–40.

Wallenda then checked the upstairs bedroom and found the body of Pamela Wilkening. She had been gagged and stabbed through the heart. Suzanne Farris lay nearby in a pool of blood, with a white nurse's stocking twisted around her neck. The detective counted eighteen stab wounds to her chest and neck. He studied Mary Ann Jordan next. She had been stabbed three times in the chest and once in the neck.

In the northwest bedroom, he found Nina Schmale, with her nightgown pulled up to her breasts and her legs pulled apart. She had also been tied and stabbed, and it looked as though her neck might be broken. Valentina Paison was found under a blue cover, lying facedown. Her throat had been cut. Tossed carelessly on top of her was the body of Merlita Garguilo, who had been stabbed and strangled.

Walking out the door and turning to the right, he saw the legs of Patricia Matusek protruding from the bathroom. She was lying on her back with her hands bound behind her. Patricia had been strangled with a double-knotted piece of bedsheet. Her nightgown had been dragged up over her breasts, and her white panties had been pulled down to expose her pubic hair. Bloodsoaked towels were strewn all over the bathroom floor.

Wallenda's hands were shaking as he left the townhouse. It was the worst crime scene he had ever witnessed.

The police immediately went to work and within hours were on the trail of Richard Speck. Cora, although heavily sedated, had managed to give an excellent description of the killer, and a nearby gas station attendant remembered one of his managers talking about a guy of the same description who had recently complained about missing a ship and losing out on a job. Police sketch artist Otis Rathel put together an uncanny likeness of Speck. Investigators took the sketch to the Maritime Union Hall and questioned the agent in charge. He remembered an irate seaman who lost out on a double booking—two guys sent for one job—and fished the crumpled assignment sheet from the wastebasket. The sheet gave the name of Richard Speck.

State's attorney Daniel P. Ward later called the manhunt for Speck the "finest bit of police work" he had ever seen. Detectives were almost immediately on Speck's trail.

After the murders, Speck moved from bar to bar, drinking himself into oblivion, not knowing that the police were on his trail. Detectives persuaded the agent at the Maritime Hall to call Speck's last known telephone number, his sister's, to tell him that he was needed to ship out. The agent connected with Gene Thornton, who agreed to try to track Speck down. He managed to find him at the Shipyard Inn and told him that the union hall had a job for him. Speck called the union hall and was told to come down for an assignment on a ship that he knew had shipped out several days before. Suspecting a trick, he told the agent that he was up north and it would take him at least an hour to get there. He never showed up.

Immediately, Speck went upstairs, packed his bags, and called a cab. He was waiting in the tavern, playing pool, when three detectives came in looking for a tall blond man with a southern accent. The bartender was no help, and Speck stayed quiet, listening and shooting pool just ten feet away from them. When the cab arrived, he refused to give the driver an address and told him he wanted to go to his sister's house, which he said was in a poor and slummy section of town. The cabbie drove north and again asked Speck for an address. Clueless, he pointed to a building that turned out to be part of the Cabrini Green housing project. He got out of the cab and watched the cabbie drive away.

Speck started walking and ended up on Dearborn Street at the Raleigh Hotel, a flophouse that had once been a luxury apartment building. A desk clerk later recalled a drunken Speck coming in with a prostitute. Just before the elevator door closed, the clerk heard the girl call the man Richard. Half an hour later, the girl came back downstairs and told the clerk that her "date" had a gun. This prompted a call to the police, and two officers from the 18th District police station showed up at the hotel at 8:30 A.M. Speck, still drunk, awoke to find two cops standing over him. He had the gun tucked into the waistband of his pants, and when asked why he had it, he told the officers that it belonged to the prostitute. When asked what his name was, he told them that it was Richard Speck. They checked his wallet and found his seaman's ID and passport, but unfortunately, not all of the police had been notified of the identity of the student nurses' killer yet. The officers questioned him for fifteen minutes and confiscated the gun but never reported it. When they left the hotel, they told the desk clerk that he was harmless.

Not realizing that Speck had narrowly escaped capture, police were searching the South Side. They managed to track him from the Shipyard Inn to the cab company, and then to Cabrini Green. But while they canvassed the housing project, Speck drank himself into another stupor. Later in the afternoon, he ran into some old friends who suggested that he hop a freight train with them and head out of town. Speck went back to the Raleigh, packed his bags, and on his way out, told the manager that he was going to do some laundry. He never returned. Just fifteen minutes after he walked out, two detectives came in and flashed a photo of Speck in front of the manager. His eyes widened, and he told the officers Speck had just left.

Oblivious, Speck headed for the Starr Hotel, a run-down dive on West Madison Street that offered temporary refuge to winos and bums. The "rooms" were nothing more than cubicles that were portioned off by plywood and had "doors" made from chicken wire. For the rate of 90 cents per night, the occupant was provided with a cot, wall locker, metal stool, and fifteen-watt bulb dangling from the ceiling on a wire. Here losers could sleep off a drunk amid the sounds of coughing and moaning and the smells of sweat, booze, and vomit. It was the last rung on the ladder for the dregs of humanity.

Tossing his bags on a cot, Speck went out to sell some of his belongings to raise money for another night of drinking. He picked up some wine at a local liquor store and several newspapers with his name and photo splashed across them. Speck stumbled back to the Starr Hotel and finished off the entire bottle of wine. He then walked down the hall to the bathroom, smashed the wine bottle, and used the broken glass to cut his wrist and inner elbow. Blood splashed onto the wall and floor, and Speck wobbled down the corridor to his cubicle. He collapsed onto the bed, still bleeding badly, and then called out to his neighbors for water and help. They ignored him.

An anonymous call was made to the police, but no patrol car was sent. Eventually Speck was taken to Cook County Hospital. The ambulance drivers ignored Speck's cries for water and missed the police bulletin on their dashboard that had the injured man's photo on it. In the emergency room, nurse Kathy O'Connor prepped Speck, and first-year resident Leroy Smith checked his wounds. Noticing something familiar about the man, he examined Speck's arm for a tattoo and saw it there, as he had suspected: "Born to Raise Hell." He compared a newspaper photo with the man and realized that he had the killer on his table.

Speck pleaded with the young man for water, but Smith grabbed him by the back of the neck and squeezed it as hard as he could. "Did you give water to those nurses?" he demanded. Smith dropped Speck's head back onto the gurney and called in a policeman who was guarding another patient down the hall. He told him that Richard Speck, the suspect in the murders, was there on the table. The stunned officer started making telephone calls, and all hell broke loose.

Richard Speck was in police custody a few hours later, and William J. Martin, a young and hard-working state's attorney, was faced with putting together and trying the case. He based most of it on the sincere and compelling testimony of Corazon Amurao, who had to be persuaded to remain in the United States long enough to secure the conviction of the monster who had killed her friends. She understandably was unhinged from her ordeal and wanted nothing more than to return to the Philippines to try to forget the horrific experience. Martin brought her mother and a cousin to Chicago for moral support and kept them in secret location away from the press. Cora's quiet testimony galvanized the courtroom and led the jury to convict Speck in just forty-nine minutes. Speck was given the death sentence for the murders.

Although he was sentenced to die in the electric chair, the Illinois Supreme Court voided the death penalty in 1971, and Speck was back in court again. This time he was sentenced to 400 to 1,200 years at the Stateville Penitentiary in Joliet. It was the longest prison sentence ever given to an Illinois inmate.

During his incarceration, Speck never admitted his guilt in the murders. He died on December 5, 1991, from a massive heart attack. His autopsy showed that he had an enlarged heart and occluded arteries, having blown up to 220 pounds by the time of his death. No one claimed his body, and it was cremated, his ashes disposed of in an undisclosed location.

But unfortunately, in 1996, Speck was back.

In May of that year, television journalist Bill Kurtis went behind the walls of Stateville prison and came back with a secret videotape, originally filmed in the mid-1980s, that showed a bizarre Richard Speck with women's breasts—apparently from hormone treatments—wearing blue panties and having sex with another inmate. Segments of the video, which also showed sex and drug orgies, were aired on the program *American Justice*, and it plunged the Illinois Department of Corrections into a major scandal. Viewers were as repulsed to see what had become of Speck as they were by his bloody crimes.

Even after death, he was still raising hell.

CHAPTER 11
The Clown That Killed

To everyone who met him, John Wayne Gacy seemed a likable and affable man. Widely respected in the community, he was charming and easy to get along with. He was a good Catholic and sharp businessman who, when not running his construction company, was active in the Jaycees and with community volunteer groups. When he was a Democratic Party precinct captain, he had his photo taken with First Lady Rosalynn Carter. He also spent much of his free time hosting elaborate street parties for his friends and neighbors, serving in community groups, and entertaining children as "Pogo the Clown." Everyone knew him as a generous, hard-working, friendly, devoted family man—but that was just the side of Gacy that he allowed people to see.

Underneath the smiling mask of the clown was the face of a depraved fiend.

John Wayne Gacy was born on St. Patrick's Day 1942 at Edgewater Hospital in Chicago, the second of three children. The Gacy children were raised in the church, and all three attended Catholic schools on the North Side. Growing up, Gacy was a quiet boy who worked at odd jobs, such as delivering newspapers and bagging groceries, and he busied himself with Boy Scout activities. He was never a particularly popular boy, but he was well liked by his teachers, coworkers, and friends from school and the Boy Scouts. He seemed to have a normal childhood, except for a series of health problems that he developed and a difficult relationship with his father.

At age eleven, while playing on a swing set, Gacy was hit in the head by one of the swings. The accident caused a blood clot in his brain, which was not discovered until he was sixteen. Between the time of the accident and the diagnosis, Gacy suffered from blackouts as a result of the clot. They were eventually treated with medication. At seventeen, he was also diagnosed with a heart ailment that led to his being hospitalized several times during his life.

In his late teens, he began to experience problems with his father, although his relationship with his mother and sisters remained strong. His father was an alcoholic who physically abused his wife and berated his children. He was an unpleasant individual, but Gacy loved his father and constantly worked to gain his attention and approval. Gacy Sr. died before his son could ever get close to him, however.

His family problems affected his schoolwork, and after attending four high schools during his senior year and never graduating, Gacy dropped out and left home for Las Vegas, where he worked part-time as a janitor in a funeral home. Lonely and depressed, he spent three months trying to get the money together to buy a ticket back to Chicago. His mother and sisters were thrilled to see him when he came back.

After his return, Gacy enrolled in business college and eventually graduated. While in school, he gained a real talent for salesmanship, and he put these talents to work in a job with the Nunn-Bush Shoe Company. He excelled as a management trainee and was soon transferred to a men's clothing outlet in Springfield.

While living in Springfield, Gacy became involved in several organizations that served the community, including the Jaycees, to which he devoted most of his efforts. He was eventually voted vice president of the local chapter and named "Man of the Year." Many who knew Gacy considered him to be ambitious, working hard to make a name for himself in the community. He was an overachiever who worked so diligently that he had to be hospitalized for nervous exhaustion on one occasion.

In September 1964, Gacy met and married a coworker named Marlynn Myers, whose parents owned a number of Kentucky Fried Chicken restaurants in Iowa. Gacy's new father-in-law offered him a position with the company, and soon the newlyweds moved to Iowa.

Gacy began learning the restaurant business from the ground up, working twelve to fourteen hours each day. Enthusiastic and eager to learn, he hoped to take over the franchises one day. When not working, he was active with the Waterloo, Iowa, Jaycees. He tirelessly performed volunteer work and made many friends. Marlynn gave birth to a son shortly after they moved to Iowa, and not long after, a daughter was added to the happy family. They seemed to have the picture-perfect life, but trouble was already starting.

Rumors were starting to spread around town, and among Jaycee members, about Gacy's sexual preferences. No one could help but notice that young boys always seemed to be in his presence. Stories spread that he had made passes at some of the young men who worked in the restaurants, but those close to him refused to believe it—until the rumors became public knowledge. In May 1968, a grand jury in Black Hawk County indicted Gacy for committing an act of sodomy with a teenage boy named Mark Miller. The boy told the courts that Gacy had tricked him into being tied up while he was visiting the man's home, and Gacy had violently raped him. Gacy denied the charges but did say that Miller willingly had sex with him in order to earn extra money.

Four months later, more charges were filed against Gacy. This time he was charged with hiring an eighteen-year-old boy named Dwight Andersson to beat up Mark Miller. Andersson lured Miller to his car and then drove him to a wooded area, where he sprayed mace in his eyes and began to beat him. Miller fought back, breaking Andersson's nose, and managed to run away and call the police. When Andersson was picked up and taken into police custody, he informed the officer that Gacy had hired him to attack the other boy.

Soon after, Gacy entered a guilty plea on the earlier sodomy charge. He received a ten-year sentence at the Iowa State Reformatory, the maximum time for the offense, and entered prison for the first time at the age of twenty-six. Shortly after he went to prison, his wife divorced him on the grounds that he had violated their wedding vows.

A model prisoner, Gacy was paroled after only eighteen months. In June 1970, he made his way back to Chicago, where he moved in with his mother and obtained work as a chef in a city restaurant.

Gacy lived with his mother for four months and then decided to move out on his own. She helped him obtain a new house at 8213 West Summerdale Avenue in Norwood Park Township. Gacy owned half of the house, and his mother and sisters owned the other half. The new two-bedroom ranch house was located in a clean, quiet neighborhood, and he quickly went about making friends with his neighbors Edward and Lilla Grexa. Within seven months of moving in next door, Gacy was spending Christmas with the Grexas. They became close friends and often gathered for drinks and card games.

In June 1972, Gacy married Carole Hoff, a newly divorced mother of two daughters. Gacy romanced her when she was most vulnerable, and she fell for his charm and generosity. She knew about his time in prison but believed that he had changed his life for the better. Carole and her daughters soon settled into Gacy's home and forged a close relationship with the Grexas. The older couple was often invited over to the Gacys' house for elaborate parties and cookouts. They were bothered, however, by a horrible stench that sometimes wafted throughout the house. Lilla Grexa was convinced that an animal had died beneath the floorboards of the place and urged Gacy to do something about it. He blamed the odor on moisture buildup in the crawl space under the house.

In 1974, Gacy started a contracting business called Painting, Decorating and Maintenance, or PDM Contractors, Inc. He hired a number of teenage boys to work for him and lied when he explained to friends that hiring young men would keep his payroll costs low. In truth, Gacy's secrets were beginning to catch up with him, and it was starting to become very apparent to those who knew him, especially his wife.

By 1975, Carole and Gacy had drifted apart. Their sex life had ended, and Gacy's moods became more and more unpredictable, ranging from jovial to an uncontrollable rage that had him throwing furniture. He had become an insomniac, and his lack of sleep seemed to make his mood swings even worse. And if his personality changes were not enough, his choice of reading material worried her even more. Carole had started to find magazines filled with naked men and boys around the house. When confronted, Gacy casually admitted that they were his. He even confessed that he preferred young men to women. This was the last straw for Carole, and she soon filed for divorce. It became final on March 2, 1976.

Gacy dismissed his marital problems and refused to let them hamper his need for recognition and success. To most people, Gacy was still the outgoing and hard-working man he always had been, and he continued to come up with creative ways to get himself noticed. It was not long before he gained the attention of Robert F. Matwick, the Democratic township committeeman for Norwood Park. As a free service to the committeeman, Gacy volunteered himself and his employees to clean up and repair the Democratic Party headquarters. Unaware of the contractor's past, and impressed by his sense of duty and dedication to the community, Matwick nominated Gacy to the street-lighting commission. In 1975, Gacy became the secretary treasurer, but his political career was short-lived. No matter how well he might have thought he was hiding his interest in young boys, rumors again began to circulate.

One of the rumors stemmed from an actual incident that took place while Gacy was working on the Democratic headquarters. According to sixteen-year-old Tony Antonucci, one of the teenagers working on the project, Gacy made sexual advances toward him but backed off when Antonucci threatened to hit him with a chair. Gacy recovered his composure and made a joke out of it. He tried to convince Tony that he was only kidding and left him alone for the next month.

Several weeks later, while Antonucci was visiting the man's home, Gacy again approached him. He tricked the teenager into a pair of handcuffs and then tried to undress him. Antonucci had made sure that he was loosely cuffed, and when he slipped free, he wrestled Gacy to the ground and cuffed the older man instead. He eventually let him go when Gacy promised not to bother him again. That was the last time Gacy ever made advances toward Antonucci, and the boy remained working for the contracting company for almost a year after the incident. Tony Antonucci did not realize how lucky he had been that day.

Others would not fare as well.

Seventeen-year-old Johnny Butkovich began doing remodeling work for Gacy's company in an effort to raise money for his racing car. He enjoyed the position, it paid well, and he maintained a good working relationship with Gacy until one pay period when his employer refused to pay him for two weeks of work. Angered that Gacy had withheld his pay, Johnny went over to the man's house with two friends to collect what was rightfully his. When confronted, Gacy refused to pay, and a loud argument erupted. Finally Johnny realized there was little that he could do, and he and his friends left.

Johnny Butkovich dropped off his friends at their homes and drove away—never to be seen again.

Michael Bonnin, also age seventeen, enjoyed working with his hands, especially doing carpentry and woodworking, and often had several different projects going at the same time. In June 1976, he had almost completed restoring an antique jukebox, but unfortunately the job was never finished. Bonnin was on his way to catch a train to meet his stepfather's brother when he vanished.

Billy Carroll, sixteen, was a longtime troublemaker who had first been in trouble with the authorities at the age of nine. Two years later, he was caught with a gun, and he spent most of his life on the streets of Chicago, making money by arranging meetings between teenage boys and adult men for a commission. Although he came from a very different background than Michael Bonnin and Johnny Butkovich, all three had one thing in common—John Wayne Gacy. Like the others, Carroll also disappeared suddenly. He left home on June 13, 1976, and was never seen alive again.

Gregory Godzik, seventeen, started working for PDM Contractors in order to finance parts for his 1966 Pontiac. The work he did for Gacy paid well, and he liked it. On December 12, 1976, Gregory dropped his date at her house and drove off toward home. The following day, the police found Gregory's Pontiac, but the boy was missing.

On January 20, 1977, nineteen-year-old John Szyc also vanished. He had driven off in his 1971 Plymouth Satellite and was never seen alive again. Szyc had not worked for PDM Contractors, but he was acquainted with Gregory Godzik, Johnny Butkovich—and fatally, John Wayne Gacy.

On September 15, 1977, Robert Gilroy, eighteen, also disappeared. An avid outdoorsman, Gilroy was supposed to catch a bus to meet friends for horseback riding. When he never showed up, his father, a Chicago police sergeant, immediately began searching for the boy. A full-scale investigation was launched, but Robert was nowhere to be found.

Gacy's web of secrets finally began to unravel with the vanishing of a young boy named Robert Piest. The investigation into Piest's disappearance eventually led to the discovery of not only his body, but also those of Butkovich, Bonnin, Carroll, Szyc, Gilroy, and twenty-seven other young men who suffered a similar fate. These discoveries horrified Chicago as well as the entire country.

Fifteen-year-old Robert Piest had disappeared mysteriously just outside the doors of the pharmacy where he worked. His mother, who had come to pick him up after his shift, was waiting outside for him when he vanished. The boy had told her that he would be back in just a minute; he was going to talk to a contractor who had offered him a job. He never returned. She began to get worried, and as more time passed, her worry turned to terror. Finally, three hours after his disappearance, she notified the Des Plaines police. Lieutenant Joseph Kozenczak led the investigation.

The first lead to follow was the most obvious one, and officers quickly obtained the name of the contractor who had offered Robert the job. Kozenczak went straight to Gacy's home, and when he came to the door, the policeman told him about the missing boy. The lieutenant also asked Gacy to accompany him to the police station to answer some questions. Gacy refused. He explained that there had been a recent death in his family and he had to attend to some telephone calls, but he agreed to come down later. Several hours later, Gacy arrived and gave a statement to the police. He said he knew nothing about the teenager's disappearance and was allowed to leave with no further questioning.

Kozenczak decided to do a background check on Gacy and was stunned when he discovered that the man had done time for sodomy with a teenage boy. He quickly obtained a search warrant for Gacy's house, and on December 13, 1978, a legion of police officers entered the house on Summerdale Avenue. Gacy was not at home at the time.

The police were shocked by what they found. Some of the items discovered in the search included a box containing two driver's licenses and several rings; a box containing marijuana and amyl nitrate pills; a stained section of rug; a number of books with homo-sexual and child pornography themes; a pair of handcuffs; police badges; sexual devices; a hypodermic needle and small brown bot-tle; clothing that was too small for Gacy; and nylon rope. The police also confiscated three automobiles that belonged to Gacy, including a 1978 Chevrolet truck with a snowplow attached and the name "PDM Contractors" on the side, a van with "PDM Contractors" also painted on the side, and a 1979 Oldsmobile Delta 88. In the trunk of the car were pieces of hair that were later matched to Robert Piest.

As the investigation continued, the police entered the crawl space under Gacy's home. They were discouraged by the rancid odor but believed it to be sewage. The earth in the crawl space had been sprin-kled with lime but appeared to be untouched. They left the narrow space and returned to police headquarters to run tests on the evi-dence they had obtained.

The police again called Gacy to headquarters and told him about the evidence that had been removed from his house. Enraged, he immediately contacted his attorney, who told him not to sign the Miranda waiver that was presented to him by detectives. The police had nothing on which to arrest him and eventually had to release him after more questioning about the Piest disappearance. They placed him under twenty-four-hour surveillance and, over the next few days, called his friends into the station and also questioned them. The detectives were unable to get any information from them that con-nected Gacy to Robert Piest, and all of his friends insisted that he simply was not capable of murder. Unable to gather other evidence, the police finally charged Gacy with possession of marijuana.

Meanwhile, the police lab and investigators were coming up with critical evidence against Gacy from the items taken from his home. One of the rings found in Gacy's house belonged to another teenager who had disappeared about a year earlier, John Szyc. They also discovered that three former employees of Gacy's had disap-peared as well. Furthermore, a receipt for a roll of film that was found in Gacy's home had belonged to a coworker of Robert Piest's, and he had given it to Robert on the day of the boy's disappearance. With this new information, the investigators suddenly began to realize the enormity of the case that was starting to unfold.

Under questioning, Gacy tearfully confessed that he had killed someone in self-defense and, frightened, had buried the body under his garage. Detectives and crime lab technicians returned to Gacy's house again. They decided to search the crawl space under the house as well as the garage, and minutes after starting to dig, they found the first corpse. Soon a full-scale excavation was taking place.

On Friday, December 22, 1978, detectives confronted Gacy with the news that digging was being done under his house. With this, the monster finally broke down. He admitted to the police that he had killed at least thirty people, and most of their remains were buried beneath the house. The first murder had taken place in January 1972 and the second in January 1974, about a year and a half after he was married. He explained that he lured his victims into being handcuffed, and then he would sexually assault them. To muffle their screams, Gacy stuffed a sock or their underwear into their mouths, and he often killed them by placing a rope or board against the victim's throat during the rape. He also admitted to sometimes keeping the corpses under his bed or in his attic before burying them in the crawl space.

The police discovered two bodies during the first day of digging. One of these was John Butkovich, who was found under the garage, and the other was in the crawl space. As the days passed, the body count grew higher. Some of the victims were found with their underwear still lodged in their throats; others were buried so close together that investigators believed they had been killed, or at least buried, at the same time.

By December 28, the police had removed a total of twenty-seven bodies from Gacy's house. Another body had also been found weeks earlier, not in the crawl space, but in the Des Plaines River. The naked corpse of Frank Wayne "Dale" Landingin had been found in the water, but at the time, the police were not yet aware of Gacy and his crimes. It was not until Landingin's driver's license was found in Gacy's house that he could be connected to the young man's murder.

The body of James Mazzara was also removed from the Des Plaines River. His underwear was found stuffed down his throat, linking him to the other victims. Gacy told the police that he had started disposing of bodies in the river because he was running out of room in his crawl space.

Much to the horror of the neighbors, the police were still excavating Gacy's property at the end of February. They had gutted the house but had found no more bodies in the crawl space. Bad winter weather had kept them from resuming the search, but they believed there were still bodies to be found. While workmen began breaking up the concrete of Gacy's patio, another horrific discovery was made: the body of a man, still in good condition, preserved in the concrete. The following week, another body was found.

The thirty-first victim to be linked to Gacy was found in the Illinois River. Investigators were able to learn his identity thanks to a tattoo on his arm, which friends of the victim's father recognized while reading a newspaper article about the grim discovery. The victim's name was Timothy O'Rourke, and he was believed to have been acquainted with Gacy.

Around the time that O'Rourke was discovered and pulled from the river, another body was found on Gacy's property, this time beneath his recreation room. It was the last body to be found on the property, and soon after, the house was destroyed and reduced to rubble.

Although the death toll had now risen to thirty-two, the body of Robert Piest was still missing. Tragically, his remains were discovered in the Illinois River in April 1979. The body had been lodged somewhere in the river, but strong winds had worked it loose and carried it to the locks at Dresden Dam, where it was finally discovered. An autopsy report showed that Robert had been strangled by paper towels being shoved down his throat.

Police investigators worked hard to identify Gacy's victims, using dental records and other clues, and eventually all but nine of the young men were identified. A mass burial was held for these unknown victims on June 8, 1981.

John Wayne Gacy's murder trial began on February 6, 1980, at the Cook County Criminal Courts Building in downtown Chicago. The defense argued that Gacy was insane and not in control of his actions, but the prosecution refuted this, stating that the murders, and subsequent disposal of the bodies, had been carried out in a deliberate manner. In their closing statements, both sides emotionally argued their case, but the jury took only two hours of deliberation to come back with a guilty verdict. Gacy had been convicted of the deaths of thirty-three young men and had the notoriety of being convicted of more murders than anyone else in American history. He received the death penalty and was sent to the Menard Correctional Center to await execution. After years of appeals, he was put to death by lethal injection on May 9, 1994.

Gacy's death brought an end to one of the most terrifying periods in Illinois' criminal history, and the mere mention of his name still manages to send a chill through the hearts of many, even after all these years.

Bibliography

Allen, John. *Legends and Lore of Southern Illinois*. Carbondale, IL: Southern Illinois University Press, 1963.

Angle, Paul. *Bloody Williamson*. New York: Alfred A. Knopf, 1952.

Asbury, Herbert. *Gem of the Prairie*. New York: Alfred A. Knopf, 1940.

Cowdery, Ray. *Capone's Chicago*. Lakeville, MN: Northstar Commemoratives, 1987.

DeNeal, Gary. *Knight of Another Sort*. Carbondale: Southern Illinois University Press, 1998.

Franke, David. *The Torture Doctor*. New York: Avon Books, 1975.

Helmer, William, and Rick Mattix. *The Complete Public Enemies Almanac*. Nashville: Cumberland House, 2007.

Keefe, Rose. *Guns and Roses*. Nashville: Cumberland House, 2003.

———. *The Man Who Got Away*. Nashville: Cumberland House, 2005.

Kobler, John. *Capone*. New York: G. P. Putnam's Sons, 1971.

Larson, Erik. *Devil in the White City*. New York: Crown, 2003.

Lindberg, Richard. *Chicago by Gaslight*. Chicago: Chicago Academy Publishers, 1996.

———. *Return to the Scene of the Crime*. Nashville: Cumberland House, 1999.

————. *Return Again to the Scene of the Crime*. Nashville: Cumberland House, 2001.

Magee, Judy. *Cavern of Crime*. Smithland, KY: Livingston Ledger, 1973.

Nash, Jay Robert. *Bloodletters and Bad Men*. New York: M. Evans and Company, 1995.

Parrish, Randall. *Historic Illinois*. Chicago: A. C. McClurg & Co., 1905.

Pensoneau, Taylor. *Brothers Notorious*. New Berlin, IL: Downstate Publications, 2002.

Quaife, Milo. *Chicago Highways Old and New*. Chicago: D. F. Keller & Co., 1923.

Rothert, Otto. *Outlaws of Cave-in-Rock*. Cleveland: A. H. Clark & Co., 1924.

Schechter, Harold. *Depraved*. New York: Pocket Books, 1994.

Sifakis, Carl. *Encyclopedia of American Crime*. New York: Facts on File, 1982.

Taylor, Troy. *Bloody Chicago*. Decatur, IL: Whitechapel Press, 2006.

————. *Dead Men Do Tell Tales*. Decatur, IL: Whitechapel Press, 2008.